MANIFESTING A NEW LIFE

Money, Love, Health and everything in between.

Compiled by Patricia LeBlanc

Manifesting a New Life: Money, Love, Health and everything in between

ISBN: **978-1516910847**

TABLE OF CONTENTS

FOREWORD!

I believe we all manifest everything we have in our lives to this very moment, yes right now as you are reading this. EVERYTHING! We are responsible for our lives and our actions and yes we ask for all of it. The Universe does deliver. Our thoughts become our action, our words, and this is your manifestation of your life!

I met Patricia LeBlanc over a year ago via social media, and when I met her I said to myself, who is this beautiful woman and where did she come from? What is Patricia all about? In due time, Patricia began to show the world her true purpose and her passion, she was walking her talk and manifesting her life and her business. It doesn't surprise me she compiled all these co-authors that are also manifesting in their fields of expertize. I feel Patricia should trademark manifesting, because when I hear that word I immediately think of Patricia.

And that is some great branding!

We can all do for ourselves, no need for the magic wand. There are many ways to accomplish getting to your manifestation. Being able to surrender is a big ingredient to manifesting. I see a lot of people asking the universe for something and then go and try to force it to happen NOW! It doesn't work this way, and yes we must do some work to get there.

So here is my analogy for all of this: We visualize a really delish pot of soup, but it just doesn't appear. We have some things to do for this pot of soup. We must go grocery shopping to buy the ingredients, chopping, preparing, adding spices and putting all of this into a large pot to cook on the stove. We let it simmer, the smell permeating through the whole house. The anticipation of the finished product and what you have built is inspiring because you know when the time has come this soup will be delish. This is how we manifest, we ask, but then we must do work, not just sit back and hope for the best. We must show the universe we are ready to receive, surrender and let go. Just like letting the soup simmer and cook to perfection.

We cannot wake up on Monday and ask for money because we are past due on a bill and expect by 5 pm that day. It just doesn't work this way. A mindset must be changed here, we must be clear about ourselves before expecting! Again, no magic wand, and this is a daily practice, not just when we need something. This is about shifting and changing.

Patricia and her co-authors provide just that. How they have arrived to their beautiful manifestation, and inspire to show how you too can accomplish the same. Ever wonder how someone can have the worst luck in the world, well it isn't luck, it what they are asking for. Ever wonder why some people just wake up and everything turns to gold for them? It is what they are asking for. We all can do this, provided we remove the static from our lives. I call this unnecessary noise and it can take us into mucky quick sand. It is YOUR CHOICE!

So my question to you, is what do you want for yourself?

Buying this book is a first step, and getting to know Patricia and her amazing co-authors is a large next step. Get out there and make it your life, no rules, boxes or anything else holding you back. The decision is all yours! It is all inside of you.

Remember, Dorothy click her ruby red shoes and said "There is no place like home!" I say home is where the heart and soul is!

Thank you Patricia, for "manifesting" this amazing book!

Kim Boudreau Smith
CEO Bold Radio Station
www.boldradiostation.com

Manifesting a New Life

Compiled by Patricia LeBlanc

DISCLAIMER

Every word in this book is based on the co-authors personal experience. The results they have achieved in their lives and shared in their chapters are not scientifically proven. I assume no responsibility for the authors sharing within these private experiences with the world. The information provided within these pages is solely your responsibility of how to incorporate it into your live. Nothing in this book is a quick fix promise. This book is solely a platform for the authors and myself to share our experiences and spread a light upon the world and give tips and advice to those who choose to take it and place it within their lives. Nothing in this book is intended to replace any medical or psychological advice. Each person's result may vary.

Manifesting a New Life

GRATITUDE AND APPRECIATION

This book would not have been possible without the support of several amazing people.

First I need to start by saying a HUGE THANK YOU to all of my amazing co-authors BettyLou, Chris, Cynthia, Elena, Gail, Jane, Jennifer, Joey, Karen, Liz, Nicola, Ramzi, Roxie, Samantha and Theresia. THANK YOU for your faith in me and for showing up willing to help make the world a better a place. I am so proud of every single one of you and I really appreciate YOU. Without you, this book would not have been possible. You all rock!!! Thank You! Thank You! Thank You!

I would not be where I am without my parents. My parents have taught me to never ever give up in life. Merci Mom et Dad pour tous les sacrifices que vous avez faits pour nous. C'est vraiment apprécié. Love you xoxo

A ma Marraine Alice, thank you so much for your words and encouragement in the last year. You encouraged me to go after my dreams and to never ever give up when others were telling me that I should quit. You told me to keep going even after people told me that I had the nerve to go after my dreams as I would never achieve them. I will always be grateful for our conversations and your amazing wisdom. Je t'aime beaucoup xoxo

Manifesting a New Life

To my cousin Kat, your support and encouragement means the world to me. You have always been there for me, no matter what. Love you xoxo.

To my close friends and inner circle, you know who you are, thank you so much for encouraging me to become a better person and to never ever give up on my dream. You have kept me going when I wanted to quit and it was quite often at times. From the bottom of my heart a huge THANK YOU! So GRATEFUL and BLESSED to have you all in my life.

To all my mentors and teachers thank you for all of your wisdom and guidance. Thank you to the naysayers as you gave me the strength that I needed at times to prove you wrong and to make my dreams come true. You have helped me to have faith in myself and to have a clear vision of what I wanted to accomplish. THANK YOU!

Thank you Kim Boudreau Smith for agreeing to write the forward to this book. I am so blessed to have you in my life as you are not only someone whom I consider to be a colleague and mentor but also a dear friend and Soul Sister. Thank you for being you and for your mentorship and friendship. You have kept me going at times. You are amazing! THANK YOU! xoxo

In the last year, I have been blessed to have meet so many people thru my various book projects, a huge thank you for helping me learn and grow to become a better person, author and compiler. Thank you for the opportunities and for showing up in the world and making it a better place.

Thank you Universe and my Angels for helping me manifest my dreams and living a happy and abundant life.

Last but not least, a huge thank you to each one of you who have purchased a copy of our book. My hope is that you will realize just how powerful you are. Your support means the world to us. I hope that you will enjoy our book and that it will change your life.

Much Gratitude and Love,
Patricia xo

Patricia LeBlanc, RMT, IARP
6 Times International Best Selling Author
Certified Abundance Attraction Coach
Registered Reiki Master Teacher
Certified Integrated Energy Therapy Master Instructor

Manifesting a New Life

INTRODUCTION

I have been very fortunate to have discovered the power of the law of attraction several years ago. This has played a huge role in my life.

You see the law of attraction is always working regardless if you are actively applying it or not. As the law says, like attract like, so it has no choice to work.

At this point, my life wasn't what I wanted it to be. It did not even come close. You see growing up, I always had big dreams and knew that I wanted to be an entrepreneur. I just never knew what type of business that I wanted to own.

After high school, I enrolled in a small business management course with the intention of either managing someone else's business or even better start my own. Instead, after I graduated, I went to University for a year and half and then started my corporate career.

When I started to study the law of attraction, I was in a very toxic job. I hated going to work. The environment was toxic. I came to hate the job that I used to love. No one was talking to each other or barely if they did. I was miserable, overweight and had major health issues. My life wasn't what I had pictured as a child.

One morning in spring of 2012, I woke up thinking I was having a heart attack. I called 911. The DR's determined it was a major case of acid reflex. It was the worst attack ever. I would get acid reflex attacks when I was stressed but never to this point. It freaked me out, but not enough to wake me up fully. Instead I started partying a little too much.

In the summer of 2012, I was in a car accident and this would become my big wake-up call. The UNIVERSE was sending me a clear signal that I needed to take back control of my life. You see I came close of dying. I needed to start living instead of being a walking zombie. I needed to stop letting fear control me and start living my life purpose. I needed to make major changes and find a way to leave my toxic job while living my life purpose.

I always knew about the law of attraction and had read the book "The Secret" by Rhonda Byrne but had pushed it to the back of my mind. My godmother and I even introduced the book to my mom back in 2010-2011. All of sudden, I would see posts, books or videos associated to the law of attraction. I took this as a sign that I needed to start studying it.

In 2013, I decided to get certified as a law of attraction practitioner and all I can is WOW!!! My life shifted and I started believing that everything was truly possible for me. I started making huge changes that were long overdue. I started by making the decision to move to Toronto. I also started taking massive action. I started manifesting amazing things into my life. I started living life on my terms. I was finally free to be me.

In November of 2013, I decided to write my 5 year business plan. In year 1, I was able to manifest things that was only supposed to happen in year 4 and 5. You see I had indicated in year 4, that I would be a published author and year 5 a Best Selling author. Well guess what? In year 1, I became a 5 time International Best Selling Author. So I know the power of the law of attraction works. I have witnessed it on a huge level. It all starts by believing in it.

I started manifesting my dream life. I started living life on my terms. I was back in control of my life. I started being me one day at a time. It took me about 2 years to rediscover my gifts and even more importantly, how to blend them together. I finally became aligned with my true self. This is when the magic started happening for me. My hope is that you find the magic too!

My wish is for you to start manifesting the life that you want and on your terms. Stop wishing for things, people and opportunities because others say you should. Start deciding for yourself what it is that you truly want. Take back control of your life. Empower yourself. You are worthy of living a better and bigger life if you choose to.

As you begin to make changes and transform your life, you will have people who will not like it. Some will come out and say you cannot achieve your goals and dreams. Others will simply be jealous as they wished that they had the guts to go after their dreams. Others do think it is impossible for them to achieve your goals/dreams, therefore, they want to stop you from failing. Do not listen to them as they will bring you down.

Listen to your heart. Listen to your intuition. Learn to how to be YOU!

Manifesting a New Life

Surround yourself with people who will encourage and uplift you. People who believe in you especially when you don't.

During challenging times, you may stop believing in yourself and your dreams.

I have been blessed to have several people who believed in me when I wanted to quit. Who told me that I needed to keep at it and make changes until I succeeded? I am so grateful now that I listened to those people. My hope is that you find the same support system as me.

I sacrificed everything to be where I am and I can now tell you, it was worth it. I did not always feel like this. My advice to you is keep moving forward every single day and surround yourself with people who are where you want to go.

Don't share your hopes and dreams with the naysayers. I have realized this the hard way. You see when you share with the naysayers, they will discourage you. This in return will bring down your energy level, to a point, you will more than likely quit.

I have someone real close to me, who doesn't believe in my dreams. Anytime that I accomplish one of my goals they will say something to bring me down. The worst is this person doesn't even do it on purpose. They just do not believe that it is possible for them, therefore, it is not possible for me either. I have stopped confiding in them as I realized I would allow it to self-sabotage myself.

Remember you are worthy of achieving your goals and dreams.

Will the journey be an easy one, more than likely not. But I can tell you at the end that it will be worth it if you play and show up fully.

You are worthy of living a happy and abundant life. You deserve it. You are doing yourself and everyone around you a disservice by not living a happy and abundant life. You were not meant to struggle, yet most of us, do on a day to day basis. There is enough abundance for everyone. So do not worry that you will take away from anyone as you will not.

In our book, you will learn different aspects of manifesting. Manifesting is simple but yet can be complex. Each co-author walks you thru their way of manifesting. There is no right or wrong way. Take what works for you and discard what doesn't. Personalize it to you.

I know it is possible to create and manifest a new life. I have done it myself. My co-authors have manifested a new life for themselves as some point of their lives. They have all walked their talk.

Always remember you deserve to live a happy and abundant life because you are worthy of it. You were not meant to struggle so make it a point today to stop doing it.

Happy Manifesting!

Manifesting a New Life

PATRICIA LEBLANC, RMT, IARP

Patricia LeBlanc inspires and motivate others to manifest their goals and dreams. Patricia is passionate about helping others to live a happy and abundant life. Using a holistic approach, she helps her clients to get out of their own way and she teaches them how to manifest their goals, dreams and desires into their life.

Patricia is an Award Winning Author, Speaker, Certified Abundance Attraction Coach, Registered Reiki Master Teacher, Certified Integrated Energy Therapy® (IET®) Master Instructor, and Certified Angel Card Reader. She is also trained and certified in Law of Attraction, Life Coaching, Life Optimization Coaching, ThethaHealing® and Realm Readings.

You can contact Patricia via:

Business Phone: 1-647-977-6987
Email: info@patricialeblanc.ca
Website: www.patriciaeleblanc.com
Website: www.manifestinganewlife.com

CHAPTER 1

HOW TO MANIFEST ANYTHING THAT YOU WANT.

By Patricia LeBlanc, RMT, IARP

"You can manifest anything that you want but, it all starts with you." Patricia LeBlanc.

For years, I was a very lost person who blocked all of my gifts. I did what I taught others wanted from me. I tried to be the perfect daughter, the perfect sister, the perfect friend, I simply tried to be perfect. I was a walking zombie and did not live up to my full potential. I was simply miserable. I was also out of alignment with myself.

Looking back, how I was able to attract anything good into my life, was a miracle.

In 2013, my life changed. I discovered the Law of Attraction and became a certified Law of Attraction advanced practitioner as well as LOA Wealth Advanced practitioner. I also became a Certified Integrated Energy Therapy (IET) Master Instructor. In 2014, I became a Certified Angel Card Reader and this was the pivotal point of my success. In 2015, I became a Certified Abundance Attraction Coach which has helped me a lot to shift my mindset to an abundant one.

In the last year, my life has transformed in ways that I never taught was possible for me. In just 14 months period, I became a 6 time International Best Selling Author, Host of a very successful international podcast, while living a happy and abundant life. I am not telling you this to brag but to let you know that if I was able to achieve everything that I did in a short period, so can YOU!

I also want to point out that it took me years to get to where I am. I had to discover who I truly was and what my life purpose was. Once I discovered both, there was no stopping me. I also needed to heal and release what was holding me back. A lot of time, we think we will manifest everything right away. That is by far the truth. Some things, we can manifest quickly, while others will take time.

I have developed my own system to manifesting and it has worked wonders for me as well as for my clients that I use this system on. This system has played a huge part to my success. I would not be where I am today without this system. I am going to share it with you with the hopes that you will implement it into your life.

My hope is that you will be able to create an abundant and happy life. Use what works for you and discard what doesn't. Make it your own.

Here are my 7 steps to manifesting anything that you want.

Step 1: Be Crystal Clear on what you want.

It is very important that you be very clear on what you want to manifest. A lot of people miss this step and then wonder why they are not getting the results that they want. Start by finding a quiet and peaceful location for you. It can be at the park, beach, top of the mountain, Nature Park, near a lake or waterfront. It can even be in a private area in your house. Whatever makes you feel joy and relaxed?

Next make certain that you have paper and pen. I have a special notebook that I write everything that I want to manifest. It has been proving that writing your goals on paper is much more powerful than writing it into a word document in your laptop, tablet or cell phone. So make it a point to write it down on paper or in a nice notebook.

Before I start working on my list, I do a combination of meditation and energy healing and I ask my angels, creator and the Universe to guide me on what I truly want and for what is for my highest good.

I then start writing it all done on paper. The more precise you are the better. Have fun with this step.

Step 2: Ask for what you want.

After you decide what you clearly want, you need to ask for it. There are several ways that you can do so. You can ask the Universe out loud. You can write it down (which I highly recommend you do also if you choose another option). You post it on social media (example if you are looking to manifest healthy body or dream vacation). You can share it with your mastermind or accountability partner. Hopefully you have at least one of them or even better both. You can turn them into affirmations or even do a vision board.

When you share it with others, make certain that they will encourage and support you no matter what! I have learned during the years that some people will try to discourage me. They do not do it on purpose but it holds me back as I feel discouraged and at times, who do I think I am wanting to manifest it into my life.

Step 3: Believe.

After you have completed the first two steps, you need to believe that whatever it is that you are manifesting is on its way to you. You need to feel it. You need to act like it is already here. You need to have faith that it will arrive in perfect divine timing as well as the way it is meant to. You see the Universe may have better plans for you or something better for you. Are you willing to refuse if it is better for you? I know I am not.

Step 4: Be in Alignment with yourself.

It is very important when you want something that it is because you truly want it. You need to be alignment with yourself. If you want something because others tell you that you should well guess what? You may end up getting it but you will not be truly happy and it will more than likely be a struggle for you. Why struggle in life when you are meant to live a happy and abundant life. I meditate and do energy self-healing sessions on myself regularly. It helps me stay aligned with myself.

Step 5: Let it go.

You need to let go of how it happen. You need to leave it up to

Manifesting a New Life

the Universe and your higher powers how it will unfold. The universe may have something better for you so learn how to let go how it will happen or when. By letting it go of the how and when, you will also be happier and have more fun manifesting.

This was really hard for me as you see everything had to go the way that I planned it to. Guess what, that rarely happen. Now that I have learned how to use the law of attraction, my life flows with ease and grace most times.

Step 6: Be open to Receive and Take Action.

It is very important to be open to receive the ideas, opportunities and people that will come into your life. You see in a lot of times, the universe will bring you ideas, opportunities and/or people into your life. When you get the amazing ideas that the universe brings to you, it is very important to act on the, right away. The reason why, is because the Universe will give the exact same idea to at least 10-15 more people. You may ask why? Well, the Universe knows that maybe 1 person will act on the exact idea that he gave others.

It is also important to take action every single day towards what you want to manifest. Perfect example, if you want to manifest 1,000,000$, then you need to start acting like you are a millionaire. Now don't go spend all of your money as you will just end up broke, but feel comfortable that you have that money. Start feeling that you are worthy of being a millionaire. How does it feel? What kind of life will you have? Who can you help? Get comfortable being in places that

30

millionaires hang out. You can even go for a coffee at the Ritz Carlton or another upscale hotel or restaurant.

Step 7: Gratitude.

It is very important to always be in a state of gratitude. Always start your day being in a state of gratitude. I wake up and say THANK YOU Universe, Creator and Angels for giving me the gift of another day. Thank you for everything that I have in my life and for the amazing gifts I will receive today. I may not say the exact same thing every day but it will always be very similar. I also write in my gratitude journal that I keep. Every night before going to bed, I will write at least 15 things that I am grateful for.

Also when someone does something nice for you like open a door for you or compliment you, say THANK YOU. It is very important to say thank you and not TY or thanks. Thank you is much more powerful than simply saying thanks or writing TY. So make it a point starting today to say THANK YOU instead of thanks or TY.

Bonus Tips to help you manifest quicker:

1-Vision Board. Vision Boards are very powerful tool to help you with manifestation. You can do just one and combine all areas of your life. Or, you can do them separately.

2- Integrated Energy Therapy (IET) Private Session. As an IET Master Instructor, I have access to a few manifesting techniques, that allows my clients to manifest quicker. I also can help you release blockages that is holding you

31

back from manifesting. When I started using IET in my private sessions the things that my clients have manifested is simply amazing! These private IET sessions can be done in person or via Skype/Phone. Contact me at www.patriciaeleblanc.com, if you would like to learn more or to book your session with me.

3- Affirmation. Affirmations are a very powerful manifestation tool that you can use. It helps to change your mindset. When you do affirmations it is very important to keep them in present tense and if possible start with the words I am. I am are the two most powerful words that you can use. Here are a few examples of affirmations: I am beautiful. I am abundant. I am worthy of abundance. I am love. I am successful.

I have provided you with the steps to my 7 step process for manifesting and included a brief overview of each step, if you would like to learn more about it or would love for me to teach you the entire system in detail, then please contact me at www.patriciaeleblanc.com/work-with-patricia for a free 30 minute strategy consultation to see if working together is a perfect fit for both of us.

I hope that you have learned a lot from my chapter as my goal is for you to manifest your dream life.

Always remember that there is enough abundance for everyone and that you truly deserve to be abundant.

Happy Manifesting!

GAIL FULLARTON

Her travels and previous experiences have taught Gail perspective. This is why she has been called a navigator, an interpreter, a translator, a weight lifter, and even a sleep provider. She acknowledges the emotional side of money, while expertly helping her clients achieve financial stability. Managing Money is more than saving and stock prices, Gail understands it's about knowing yourself, what might be holding you back and how to inspire you to change. Her background in education, training, and corporate management give her unique insights that encourage and nurture long lasting financial success.

You can connect with Gail at:

gail.fullarton@hotmail.com
@MyPinkPortfolio
www.facebook.com/pages/Gail-Fullarton
www.thepinkportfoliogroup.com
www.advisingwomenonwealth.com

CHAPTER 2

THE STABLE TABLE – IF A TABLE ISN'T STABLE HOW USEFUL IS IT?

By Gail Fullarton

Yummy I hear you say – the Financial Chapter. In this book you will read a lot about how to manifest your wealth, and it's my privilege to provide you with some solid tips on actions you need to practice for when the universe does decided to deliver. Then you'll know how to receive your new wealth wisely. Remember manifesting without actions - you're just dreaming, so read on and discover your actions.

When I am working with clients and strategizing with them on their wealth, the first thing I need to understand is, 'What is your emotional attachment to money'? There are many emotions that we unconsciously attach to money and even the idea of money. Guilt, anger, confusion, repression, betrayal, and fear are just a few and usually the most common.

Through the process I follow, we change the relationship you have with money into emotions such as freedom, security and independence. Only when you have worked on and successfully changed your self-limiting beliefs will your manifestations result. So instead of running away from debt or lack, I'd like you to start running towards your inspirational wealth.

If you have a detachment with your money then you're not in sync with your life's path. For example, I was working with a lovely girl (let's call her Lucy) in her early twenties who was in debt. She loved to pick up the tab for dinners when out with friends. Lucy's underlying emotion was lack of and it stemmed from her parents financial situation. While she was so afraid of ending up in the same situation as her parents, her pride and image was over compensating - Lucy was over spending, and she was spiraling. I was so happy she realized she needed help and was referred to me. We followed my Stable Table process and I came to understand she so wanted to feel secure and validated. Through various techniques we were able to change her mindset and she had some rather large 'aha' moments. These were repeated patterns throughout her life and her money issues were just one of the many symptoms. I am very happy to say her financial situation has changed and surprise surprise - so has her life. She no longer is the follower in the group and those friends who could not support her taking charge of her life, she no longer sees. Lucy understands the true meaning of acceptance: starting with herself and that she is the provider of her own security. Watching her Money grow in her accounts and seeing her vision materialize has helped her understand she is not her parents and she is the key holder to her life.

Dealing with the Energy and Emotion of my clients is complemented by a comprehensive financial review and could be called a holistic approach to dealing with the energy and emotion of money.

Validation does not equal money, and money does not equal validation. Let's just get that out there, yet we focus so much on it. There is too much focus on money, and not enough on the lifestyle and experiences it can afford you. I help my clients have a better understanding of what money is to them and not from how the market doing.

The freedom, security, peace and of course happiness that money can provide depends on your attachment to money. Too many financial advisors solely look at the planning of money and miss the emotional attachment their clients have with money. I find you can't aspire one without understanding the other.

When narrowing your focus on to a more abundant life, focus on the following;

An experience, a novelty that means something to you, something that will allow you to spend time with those who make you happy and invest in others. I know that writing a check for $1,000,000 is wonderful and worked for Jim Carey, but I have found for most people that it doesn't evoke the right emotion and the key word is 'emotion'.

Which brings me to a friend who needed $5000 to attend a conference in Chicago and she was focusing on manifesting $5000. It wasn't until we talked about the conference, what she was looking forward to experiencing and of course visiting Chicago did I see the twinkle in her eye and she felt it too. She realized she had been visualizing the wrong thing and instead of looking at the check on the fridge for $5000, she needed to feel the emotion of being at the conference. Guess what, contracts and potential clients began popping up all over the place and she got to participate in the conference.

So going back to the title of this chapter 'Stable Table' refers to my financial review approach, a quick 'how to take control of your finances'.

So why do I use the visual of your kitchen table at home? It's the central place in the home where everything happens; intimate coffee chats with those close to you, baking birthday cakes for those you love and of course ice cream at midnight – alone. I like to say the good, the bad, and the ugly of life happens on your kitchen table. So it needs to be strong and stable enough to take what's thrown at you.

I divide your life into 4 parts and this is where I use the 4 legs table analogy, the Stable Table approach, it's the simple, yet complete process. The 1st quarter is your emergency reserve, 2nd your mid-term goals, 3rd your long term and retirement and finally how insurance can provide a security net to catch you when life happens and plan for future generations. All your legs need to be equally stable and supported. Otherwise it's wonky.

Short term – do you have 3- 6 months of liquidity? By this I mean, savings. It can be different for each of us. This really is your emergency fund and should be respected and kept for 'I need a new roof', not "oh, I want that ….." (Purse, shoes, gadgets etc.)

Liquidity, can also be different for each of us. It could be cash in the bank earning interest (without penalty for withdrawal), a line of credit and even money sitting in your account.

Mid-term goals, start saving for the life you want to lead, putting $50 a week towards the trip you want to take in July,

Manifesting a New Life

by focusing on the trip (remember Chicago), the $50 will start showing up. (I use $50 just as an example, a guide line would be more like 10%)

Long term goals - paying off the house and retirement, so again, start putting money away. It's much easier to do the younger you are. Get in to the habit of saving and visualize what it's for – not just 'it's for retirement', but where do you want to live, who's with you and what are you laughing at, dancing too, etc.?

I understand that we tend not to think of retirement until it's upon us, however getting into the habit of saving earlier will help you have a healthy relationship with money. Not saving early enough can be seen as self-sabotage, so why are you holding your freedom ransom?

Good tip – if you're living at home and haven't moved out yet, look at the money you are saving by not paying the full price of rent and put it in a savings account. What you're really doing is getting used to live on a realistic amount of money and when you do move out, 1- you can handle what's left after rent has been paid and 2- you have some savings.

Win Win!

The final quarter is Insurance and I'm not just talking life insurance but living benefits too. What kind of safety nets do you have? I view safety nets as something that allows you to live life to its fullest and should be an inspiration to enjoy life rather than be afraid of what might happen. For example here in Canada winters are cold and snowy and I liken having insurance to having winter tires on your car. They give you the confidence to drive and go out and live during the winter, greatly diminishing your slipping, sliding and spinning.

So an example of The Stable Table in action would be 'Jenna'. She was in a place she really did not expect to be; divorced and alone. She had a nice sum of money from her settlement, and was frittering it away as she really didn't want the money. She was associating it with the hurt and betrayal she felt for her ex. One of the first things she had done as a single girl was to purchase a new Lexus to help booster her self-confidence and show him (Jenna had always wanted a Lexus).

Needless to say the emotion of the purchase reverted back to the origin of the money and through self-sabotage she was rear-ended. The car was a write off.

Through our conversations, Jenna began to realize she'd been in a cycle of pleasing everyone else. And where did that get her; alone in her thirties. Not only did Jenna need a financial plan, therapy was needed too.

Using the Stable Table we figured out what she really wanted in life was 'A New Start'. So a quest began and she started to figure out what she liked and who she really was, and how her settlement could be so much more than a reminder of the pain of her former life. In the interim stage we kept 3 months' worth of salary in her bank account and invested the rest in risk appropriate funds – some of which was ear marked for a home (she just wasn't sure where yet). She was approved for living benefits and life insurance and so even though she was alone she didn't need to rely on anyone should something happen to her – phew! That was six months ago and while she's still transitioning into the beautiful independent soul we call Jenna, she's still not quite sure what kind of home she wants. Jenna is however inspired by the growth of her nest egg and the potential life it will afford her.

Tip #1 - To get the results you want, you need action and using my Stable Table approach is going to get the action started. You are also going to need to dig deep and figure out what your relationship is to money – it wants to be valued and respected.

Tip #2 - In order to be ready for the money to flow, you need to get your house in order and I literally mean get your house/home in order – life clutter is financial clutter – tidy it!

CHRIS SPINK, RN, DCH

Chris Spink is the founder of ManifestYourDesires.com. He is a fully trained and qualified Registered Nurse, Counsellor, Clinical Hypnotherapist and Law of Attraction Life Coach. Chris is passionate about empowering others so they can enjoy a life of increased prosperity, loving relationships, vibrant health and blissful joy. He helps people master the principles of the *Law of Attraction*, and feeling good so they can manifest their goals, dreams and desires. Chris is currently creating powerful new courses so you can replace your negative beliefs with positive and create your life the way YOU want it to be.

Website: manifestyourdesires.com

Facebook Page: www.facebook.com/ManifestYourDesires

LinkedIn: www.linkedin.com/in/manifestyourdesires

Email: chris@manifestyourdesires.com

Chapter 3

FEELING GOOD IS THE KEY TO EVERYTHING YOU WANT.

By Chris Spink, RN, DCH

Did you know that the most important thing you can do for yourself and the world is choosing to feel good? Feeling good is the key to whatever you want to be, do or have. You are the creator of your reality and the formula for creating everything you desire is simple:

Feel good + Law of Attraction = All Your Dreams and Desires. Everyone wants to feel good and if you can choose to feel good first without changing your conditions, you will have attained manifesting mastery. Instead of needing the world and people around you to change before you feel good, you can feel good and watch the world change to match your good feeling.

We live in an energy based universe with energy based laws. The Law of Attraction is one such law which draws to you the essence of whatever you predominantly focus your attention on. Some people think that the law of attraction is only working when they get what they want. They don't realize that it is always working, always responding to the majority of the vibration you are expressing. So if the majority of your thought and feeling is focused on feeling good then everything you want will manifest. Have you ever noticed when you or others are feeling good and are "in the zone" that everything seems to flow easily and everything works out? In contrast have you noticed when you or others don't feel good, frustrated or angry then things continue to go wrong? Whatever you focus on is what you get.

The next thing that is helpful in manifesting everything you want is to know that you will never be complete or finished and happily you never will be. Imagine getting everything you want right now and not wanting anything else. That would truly be the end of this wonderful journey for you. Fortunately we are eternal beings, that's why we will never get to a place where we are totally complete and so we can't get it wrong.

Also remember that the true essence of who you are is an extension of the nonphysical, expressing as form in physical reality. You are perfect and worthy as you are; all you are doing here is having an experience of physical reality where you get to create whatever you choose. When you get what you want, you will simply want something more. Life continues to expand and grow. Your life is supposed to feel good to you because you have deliberately chosen to be here to create your dreams and desires. Relax and know that all is well.

There are three basic steps to manifesting or creating your reality.

Step One

As we live our lives, there are occasions when a negative experience occurs. The negative experience provides us with

43

the contrast we need to help us recognise that this is an experience we don't want, this automatically, tells us what we do want. It's not always easy to know exactly what we desire until we experience what we don't want. For example, if someone is angry or mean to us, our automatic desire is for that person to be happy and kind to us, or if we face difficulty because we don't have enough money, love or happiness, this reveals to us we would prefer our lives to be more abundant in money, love or happiness.

Step Two

After we experience what we don't want and acknowledge our true desire. Your Inner Being (the larger all-knowing part of you) instantly responds to what you want? Your Inner Being holds everything you have ever wanted in a vibrational reality and is ready to bring it to you in the perfect way. This vibrational reality is waiting to become physical reality and manifested into your life, as soon as you follow step three.

Step Three

This is your only active role in creating what you want. It is your role to align vibrationally with your dreams and desires. In other words, you need to find a way to get happy and feel good, no matter what, to attract what you desire into your life. Your Inner Being will then send you thoughts, feelings, situations and people at the perfect time for you to receive exactly what you want in the perfect way.

Step one is automatic when we come up against what we don't want we ask for what we do want.

Step two is taken care of by our Inner Being, and therefore, we do not need to do anything.

Step three requires us to feel good no matter what is happening. This is the essential key to manifesting your dreams and desires

The easiest way I have found to be happy and feel good, is to wake up every day with the intention to feel good. The momentum of certain thoughts from the day before has stopped while you sleep, so this is the best time of day to set this intention. When you start your day feeling good, focusing on things that you appreciate, the law of attraction brings you more thoughts that feel good. When you practice appreciation for what is working in your life and notice things around you that you appreciate, everything begins to look brighter and more enjoyable. Every morning look for reasons to feel good. Find positive things from your past. Look for positive things happening right now. Look for positive things that you want in the future. Smile a lot. It is your natural state to be a happy person. It's natural for you to love and to laugh.

Using these principles, my wife and I became financially free and could choose whether to work or not, in less than five years. Before this we lived on very little and sometimes needed welfare to get by, although generally we felt good in our lives and didn't worry about money or not having enough.

We didn't know it at the time but this was the perfect mindset from which to attract wealth and well-being into our lives. We were not actually looking to become rich or wealthy, we were just living a comfortable and happy life, feeling as if we had everything we needed.

45

Manifesting a New Life

Over the next five years we managed to build a large property portfolio with some hard work and a lot of allowing. Now, with hindsight, I see that it was our feel good attitude and beliefs around money that attracted our new-found wealth. We were in the ideal emotional state to attract wealth and did so with relative ease.

Your feelings are your guide to your vibrational alignment with your Inner Being. So how you feel tells you whether you are aligned with what you want or not. If you feel good you are in perfect alignment. If you don't feel good then you are out of alignment. How you feel shows you what your present point of attraction is, in other words, what you will be creating next in your life. So if you feel anxious, frustrated, discouraged, inferior, worthless or afraid, that is your current point of attraction, if you feel joyful, happy, healthy or loving then that is your point of attraction, and is what you will manifest next in your life.

Feeling good is a choice, not a reaction to circumstances. You might ask, 'how do I feel good when something is happening that makes me feel bad?' The answer to that question is that you can't look at a situation that feels bad and expect to feel good. Instead, you need to take your focus away from the 'not so good stuff' and deliberately place it on better feeling thoughts.

Your dreams and desires will manifest when you make how you feel the most important thing in your life. Care more about how you feel than what is happening in your life and you will see the results manifesting quickly. But please don't just believe me. Improve the way you feel and see for yourself if this works or not; either way if you wind up feeling better, wouldn't that alone be worthwhile? You can choose to feel better any time you wish, just choose a thought that feels better.

Here are some additional tips that will help you feel good:

- Meditate and relax
- Find more things that please you
- Get outdoors more often
- Breathe more consciously
- Walk/exercise more often
- Have more fun
- Make time to pursue interests you feel passionate about

You will only see the evidence you want when you actually put into practice the principles of the law of attraction in a way that changes your reality, and that is, by choosing to feel good most of the time.

Feeling good most of the time can be challenging for most of us. Shifting one's mindset and reversing your negative self-talk is not always easy, but I promise you that if you practice these things and start to feel good through choice not through reacting to circumstances, you will start to see the results in your life and you will be choosing to feel good along your journey. What could be better than that?

47

Manifesting a New Life

CYNTHIA SAMSON

Cynthia Samson is an enthusiast projects propulsor who dedicates her researches on how to live a life at its fullest by combining and expand spiritual and physical potentials.

Born with an intuitive strength and a practical-mind approach, she worked for 15 years with organizations around the world in project management and process improvement, designing and implementing effective game changer strategies (North-America, Europe, and Japan). Investing the last decade in R&D and training with masters in metaphysic, spirituality and NLP, Cynthia offers unique training, mastermind and mentoring programs for men and women to connect and embody their essence, truth and inner power.

www.UniqueMomentandSpace.com
uniquemomentandspace@gmail.com

Chapter 4

STOP ASKING QUESTIONS START ASKING THE TRUTH

By Cynthia Samson

The first time I heard my voice saying:

I ASK THE TRUTH and LOVE INVITES ME TO WELCOME AND RECOGNIZE THE OBVIOUSNESS OF THE TRUTH.

I knew, deep within every cell of my body, that I just entered into a whole new area; a place I had never been before. This was the PASSWORD, THE MASTER KEY to unlock what is VITAL and ESSENTIAL in my life, and to manifest it beyond anything I ever thought possible.

I OWN my LIFE.

I started to play again. I found that sacred place inside me where peace, faith, joy of creation reside. I build a strong and grounded foundation of love within my body.

I NOW assume my calling and my purpose on this planet. I experiment and enjoy manifesting as a natural expression of who I am.

LOVE MY LIFE NOW.

This was THE REVELATION for me! I was a women who had been praying to die almost every day of her life. I felt like a fish outside the water who did not belong to this world.

The GAME OVER POINT and TURNING POINT came in June 2013.

I decided to pull the handbrake on my life... I had enough! I don't go any further! This is over! This is it! I SURRENDER! I DON'T KNOW ANYMORE!

At that moment, I truly believed (my mind actually believed it!) that I had done everything possible to "achieve" self-realization and happiness. How could this be? Even with all my will, my background, my knowledge, my experiences and my continuous training in self-development that I could have found myself in a loop of "CHECKMATE"?

No matter the strategy, that loop was playing with me, like in the movie 'Groundhog Day'.

From an external standpoint, I was a strong, determined, achieving, wealthy women, but, deep inside, I was seeking for a meaning to life itself.

I understood the laws of the universe, metaphysics, neuroscience (I thought!) but, I was far away from my heart, my body and life itself. I was locked into a prison made of glass.

Manifesting a New Life

I defined myself by my career: a business project manager, built to achieve goals, to find opportunities and resolve problems that came my way. I achieved my goals. I travelled the world, worked on great innovative projects...but, joy, authentic love, peace, gratitude, fulfilment and health were terribly missing in the equation.

Something I knew (even though I said I DON'T KNOW ANYMORE): the quality of life is linked to the quality of questions asked. Questions attract answers, creating manifestations and synchronicities.

I was missing something. I had spent so much time swimming in the mud of my mind's complex analysis to find questions that I should asked myself to manifest my dreams.

There was crystal clear evidence during that morning in June...I can drill down like that for many years and still find myself in that mind "out of life" loop.

So I STOPPED right there and JUST SAID: "GAME OVER". I REMAINED IN SILENCE and my mind shut down for a while.

Then, another question came up (I trained my brain for so many questions)...So I asked:

What is the most powerful, simple and loving question to ask myself to realize who I AM, to manifest both inner and outer peace, joy, belonging, faith, confidence, purpose, fulfilment, abundance and wealth in all situations, all aspects of my life? (Long question, of course, from my mind. At the same moment, I was into a state of presence at 100%).

The answer came straight from my heart: ASK THE TRUTH!!!

POWERFUL and yet, at the same time, it FREAKED ME OUT!

Am I ready for it?

In a second, my mind brought up an image of a judge asking me: Do you swear to tell the truth, the whole truth, nothing but the truth. STOP! What's that!

What is the truth anyway?

I meditated on the truth for many months, like a newborn making her first steps. I had no reference point, no GPS, few human being models. I fell and stood up many times.

Then, one day, EUREKA!

The LEVER, the PROPULSER AFFIRMATION through the voice of my spouse came:

LOVE INVITES YOU TO WELCOME AND RECOGNIZE THE OBVIOUSNESS OF THE TRUTH.

This was THE INVITATION to discover, to welcome the mystery of the truth, unadulterated and simple. I didn't need a user guide to encompass truth; just accept the invitation of LOVE to guide me through to it.

Super!!! HOW DO I DO THAT? (My beautiful mind!)

Manifesting a New Life

I simply took the DECISION to make it my practice, my R&D of life and manifestation. I decided and committed to play FULL IN, 100%.

This is how I got started, each day, at each moment by simply saying: "I ask the truth and love invites me to recognize the obviousness of truth." I declared it, sang it, danced it, laughed it, breathed it, cried it, embodied it, loved it, lived it...LISTENED to it.

Surprisingly, I discovered that truth liberates, raises level of energy, expands clarity and inner power. And, since the common point of all the spheres of my life is 'me', all the spheres of my life got ignited.

During the following weeks and months of mastering my new practice, my mind started to notice many strange things while my body was delighted.

I started to admit that I am unique, that I have my place on this earth; no fight, just owning it. My contribution is important! My role: to create. I can count on myself and find support everywhere. Seems pretty logical!!!...However there is a huge difference between understand it from mind's perspective and vibrate it in every single cell of your body thru the perspective of the heart.

There was more...The universe participates to my fulfilment! Its radar is larger than mine, so it surprises me with new experiences that expand the field of possibilities of fulfilment. That's where the real fun begin!!! Ho Yes!!

At the same time, truth through love showed me behaviours, false beliefs that were obstacles to my fulfilment. Truth opened my eyes on my deepest legitimate needs...

Truth taught me how to overcome self-sabotage;

On many occasions, I have run away from great opportunities; I wasn't enough, I thought. With that practice, when self-defeating behaviours or feelings of shame kicked in, in a second I said I ask for truth and LOVE invites me to welcome and recognize the obviousness of truth.

Each and every time, truth came in a second. Truth is a divine right, available anytime, anywhere...One day, Truth came through a question!

This is something you may experience in this practice. Truth reveals itself in the NOW, in short simple words, images, sounds, intuitions, inner states. The way you experience it is unique. For me, it's a deep peace in my heart expanding in my body. Truth is PRESENCE.

Sometimes, truth asks questions. Yep! Questions that you never asked yourself before...

ARE YOU READY TO LOVE YOURSELF? ARE YOU READY TO ACCEPT LOVE COMPLETELY?

(Silence)

At that moment, I saw an infinite abundance available for me, NOW. The level of manifestation in both my inner and outer life was in direct proportion with the level of love I gave to myself, I accepted to receive and I accepted to give.

Opening my arms wasn't enough. The question showed me to recognize that I AM LOVE. Truth, abundance, energy, love, everything is available because it's already within me, my soul, heart, spirit, body, DNA; all of it.

LOVING MYSELF ALLOWS THE UNIVERSE TO PARTAKE IN MY CONTRIBUTION TO THE WORLD, it manifests far more than only for myself.

Not accepting to LOVE MYSELF COMPLETELY was a selfish ego trip that blocked manifestations in my life. OUCH!!!

MAKING THE DECISION to LOVE myself COMPLETELY ignited my inner fire (I made the decision and informed my body about it... the body materializes decisions) in connection with my essence.

This led to an amazing side effect: expansion of my intuitive gifts. It translated into my life by attracting more and more people with a desire to connect to their essence, their mission and manifest it.

I kept my intuitive gifts private for many years, few people knew about it. Being identified as a business project leader for an international corporation, I was afraid that I would lose my credibility.

It was not about me anymore, it was about service.

And, something great happened.

I never been filled with more joy, love, deep sense of presence and belonging to life. I experimented in all my body that being at service offering my natural talents (that I enjoyed...and this includes my intuitive gifts), helped others and, by doing so, manifestation and abundance increased in their lives as well as mine.

I am an apprentice on this path...this is the best way to remain opened. I am blessed with friends that chose truth as a way of life and it feels so good to see all of us blossom.

Lately, truth asked me: TIME...WHAT DOES IT MEAN FOR YOU?

Manifesting a New Life

JENNIFER LOW

If you are finding yourself seeking a new path in life yet can't figure out how to get out of "stuck", then Jennifer is the right ally for you!

This multi-talented and creative woman will shine her inspirational light onto your path and will guide you step by step towards clarity and results.

She will show you how to go from something that doesn't work, to something that does, and more importantly to something that will fit more harmoniously with who you naturally are.

Jennifer is a certified NLP coach, teacher, and mom.

Website: AnAuthenticU.com
FB page is An Authentic U

CHAPTER 5

CLEARLY.... I HAVE THE POWER TO MAKE IT HAPPEN

By Jennifer Low

The art of manifesting starts with one primary ingredient: knowing what you want!

There is immense power in clarity. Anyone who is successful at anything in their life has been blessed with the insight of knowing what they want, the capacity of self-discipline, and the ability to pursue their desire with a razor sharp focus and a graceful rhythm.

I was reminded of this back in 2008. My therapist asked me to write a list of my perfect man. At first I thought she may be joking.... After all, we all know there is no such thing as a perfect man, right?! I reminded her of this two appointments later, and admitted that this was my reason for not wanting to waste my time with this. I figured this exercise would be futile and useless.

"Be careful", she kindly responded. "If you don't make that list, Fate will bring you something you did not ask for!" I can't explain what happened next, but in that instant I received this "threat" as a 15 lbs. medicine ball right to my chest.

The next time I was in her office, I arrived with a list in hand. She was very keen on seeing it. I had based the items on my list on the many male friends I have had in my life, as well as on my interactions with them and the positive influence they have had on me.

From one friend I was getting lightness, happiness and FUN! We always laughed and giggled when we were together. There was a spontaneity between us I truly enjoyed. So I took that. This person was also very kind and caring which made me feel good about myself. I wrote these characteristics on my list.

I was learning how to fly at the time and my instructor and I had built quite an intimate 'brain' connection. It was soft, gentle and easy. It was simple and free flowing. I really appreciated that. It was a relationship built on trust, respect and sensitivity to energy. In the cockpit, our interaction was mentally seamless. We always worked from the same page.

I applied that to my list! It was important for me to have a perfect teammate: someone who would pick up where I left off.

I even added the best qualities of what filled some of my best moments with my ex-husband. I wanted someone who liked to explore, someone smart, curious, inquisitive, adventurous without needing to seek extreme excitement to feel fulfilled. I have always been attracted to "different" and needed someone who thought outside the box.

My therapist took the list and started:

Manifesting a New Life

"You want someone kind. Are you kind?"
"Yes!" I answered confidently.
"You want someone who is smart. Are you smart? "
"Well YES!" I responded with conviction.
And so she kept going, item by item down the list.

Her purpose for this list was two fold: the first was to demonstrate to me that commonality is good! "Girls in their teens and twenties look for opposites; women in their thirties and onwards look for similarities." If you are looking for someone long term wouldn't it in fact make sense to choose someone who loves to do the things you also like to do?

Harmony is stressless.

The second purpose for that list was to provide me with a clear working dream map. This allowed for no second best, for no second guessing, and no "settling".

This list showed me what I wanted and what would make me happy.

The list was a work-in-progress between 2008 and 2014. I got to a point in my life where I was definite about not willing to compromise anymore. This man had to be perfect for me or I was resolute to stay single. Now I just had to make sure I knew what perfect meant to ME.

Making sure I started with the end in mind, my list underwent a new movement, a new organizing. I looked at this like a business building exercise: reverse engineering! I had now categorized it in layers. The first one was about deal breakers. This is the non-compromise category. This person

MUST have "this and that" or he's not getting my time of day. These included things like strong friendship and not snoring. A friend of mine laughed at me when he found out about the snoring "You are being way too picky", he said. But I'm a long term thinker you see… and if I'm going to share a bed with someone, it's because I'd like to. And for a very long time. As far as I was concerned I was getting a second chance at looking for a great lifelong partner. I also value my sleep very much and I don't want to be one of those couples who sleeps in separate beds for the sake of sleep sacredness. Our life cycle is too short not to enjoy togetherness.

The next section was "very important factors". These comprised all the personality traits. For me it meant someone who pays attention to detail, who is optimistic, who has similar philosophies as I do, who respects me, who is kind to me and to others, etc.

The third and last section was all about the details that make up his everyday life. Where he lives, his current marital status, if he has kids, what type of work he is involved with, how he earns his income, and so on. All the things that make up who he is now.

Sure enough, it is always when you don't entertain it as a forced and planned forethought that manifesting happens so naturally and beautifully. So much so that it even catches YOU by surprise at times. That is to say manifestations, especially when you least expect it, come from the most unlikely places. Your job is to set the intention; the how is never yours to know. I often remind myself that I am the one who creates my life. Every moment of it!

I met my current partner 2 years ago. We were volunteering our time for an event. Remember… I was single at the time. I was always on the lookout with one antenna up and one cocked sideways. Of the entire group, he was the one that looked least attractive to me. He was too quiet and he was also not physically my type at all. We were paired together for guest registration that first morning of the event. I thought to myself: "Hmmm… What do I do with this? I might as well engage him a little since I have to work with him all weekend." He was lost in his own momentum that day. I left him alone.

We volunteered again together 6 months later. It was then that we started conversing through Facebook. We kept showing up at the same events and got to know each other better. We became best friends and then… we fell in love!

Throughout our friendship I had noticed many things about him I liked very much. Slight subtleties of peaceful commonalities. Even though I slowly discovered how well he fit my list, I had never considered a union for he was so much younger than me. What I had failed to pay attention to is that even though my list had undergone a fine tooth clean up, I had forgotten over the years to change one thing: his age!

True to form, I created what I wanted and I received exactly that.

We are all deliberate creators of our own lives. We have all been dulled to believe that living is restricted to status quo.

What we fail to remember is that each of us hold the most powerful golden key to any and all treasures: the power to create DELIBERATELY with our mind. We are always creating with our minds: it is either creating intentionally, which is most favorable, or it is creating by default. The good, the bad, the ugly, the sensational. It's all a creation by us.

Choose your thoughts wisely...

In my opinion, athletes are some of the luckiest people on earth. They get it right at an early age. They set themselves up with a guide (a mentor) who will teach them this delicious recipe of quickly assessing, tweaking through small adjustments, and visualizing their "play", thereby intentionally and deliberately creating the outcome they desire. Through those action steps they experience success.

I encourage you to be your own magic-makers, to keep creating the life you want, in your head, on paper, and in application so it can truly become your reality. This is a repeatable formula, applicable in any field.

I wish you prosperity and success in creating and manifesting your perfect partner, in uncovering your authentic self, in seeking out the right path for you, and for the awesome opportunities coming your way.

Keep your arms open so as to receive it all!

Thank you, Universe!

Manifesting a New Life

BETTYLOU NELSON

BettyLou Nelson is a conservative version of the well-known Fruitcake Lady giving wise advice to women. She co-authored two other books including international bestseller, "Sexy Secrets to a Juicy Love Life" and is the author of "Top Secrets to Find and Keep Him for Mature Women Only" They are blueprints for action to find your true love. They are not merely commentaries but insightful strategic plans written in light-hearted good taste. She is engaged at age 71 to a wonderful man and happily living in Florida. An acclaimed university trained educator and writer who has been given Expert Writing status by a well-known publisher.

Phone: 352-399-5929

Email: betty.nelson@comcast.net

Location: Florida, USA

Time Zone: EST

Website: http://fabulouswomenover50.com/

Facebook: https://www.facebook.com/BettyNBoope

Pinterest: https://www.pinterest.com/bettylounelson/

EZine Articles: http://ezinearticles.com/?expert=Betty_L_Nelson

Skype: bettynels43

Chapter 6

SECRETS AND SMART MOVES FOR WOMEN TODAY

By BettyLou Nelson

Meeting men is easy once you get the hang of it. Practice smiling and greeting them in stores, waiting in line, etc. Start making casual, fun, chatty conversation with men you see throughout the day. If someone you would like to meet is talking with the guys, catch his eye and look away. A few minutes later, catch his eye again, hold it for a second, this time smile and look away. Go to the ladies room so he wonders where you are. On the way back, confidently walk right passed him, catch his eye, hold it and smile and return to your friends. He will get the message and will likely approach you. Or you may ask the hostess or a friend to introduce you. When he approaches, start the conversation by tossing him a crumb and say nice tie or nice watch, etc. He will take it from there......

Attitude and Timing is everything. A woman with confidence is very intoxicating to a man. She is a challenge and it gives him a chance to pursue her. When he calls for a date, say you only have two days open next week. Never be too available. Let him think you have a great life and that others are

The only real question to ask on your first date is to ask him if he believes in marriage. You are not asking if he would marry you. You are simply asking if he believes in marriage. He may say not now because of school or other things or that he does believe in marriage and family. Bingo, you have your answer right away without waiting for months. Some of us don't have time to dilly dally. Be very honest with yourself and what you want in a man upfront. If you are looking for a long term relationship, say so, clearly and sweetly.

Don't worry if he doesn't call for a day or two. Don't call him. Some men get temporarily distracted or just need a break to think. Keep calm, go out with friends and let the answering machine take his call so he knows you are not waiting by the phone. You have a life!!! Anxiety is simply a signal for you to prepare. If you can't do anything else, make a plan and a strategy to handle the steps you need to take. That will take the stress off. Men like a woman to look like a desirable woman. Pretty heels are proven to increase your chances of a date and don't forget to smile!

Is chemistry and attraction important? Does your heart beat faster when you see his car drive up? It is, indeed, very important for a long term relationship to succeed. The excitement of the first year will calm down and this basic attraction will be the glue that holds you together long term.

Don't let money or other things be the determining factors or you will live to regret it. Don't let sex make you stupid.

Having sex too soon prevents your ability to clearly assess him. Don't drop your guard before you drop your panties, ladies. Put him to the acid test of the 90 day no sex rule. This quickly weeds out the sports fisherman from the potential keepers. And wisely use these 90 days to interview him to determine if he meets your needs and values for the coveted job of your mate. After all, you are likely trusting him with your heart and your life. Think like a man. Most men don't date just one woman. And companies don't interview just one person for a job. If you are dating more than one man, this makes it easier to graciously let him go! Make this a fun process. Don't drill him. You do the asking and don't tell all during the first few dates. Be careful, some men will use the 90 days as a challenge to break you down. So don't put yourself in risky situations where you are frequently alone.

There is a safe, simple way to stop seeing a man you have dated a few times but realize he is not what you want. Don't do this in person as it may be unsafe. Call him and sweetly say that you enjoyed his company but it is not working for you. If he asks why, simply keep saying it is not working for you. Don't give him reasons he can argue with. Say you must go and hang up. If he calls again, do not return his calls.

Here is a good way to test his interest in you. After dating for a time and it appears his interest is waning a bit but you still like him, pull away just a little. Say you are not available a time or two when he wants to see you. If he becomes more attentive and you are comfortable with the relationship, good, if not, let him go. Think like a man does. Sweetly put yourself first. He does. A good man thinks in terms of fairness and so should you.

Be totally honest with yourself and write down the absolute most important things you need in a man. Men appreciate knowing these things upfront. Financially, a women's best bet is to require that a man's income is equal to or slightly more than hers. You must talk about division of finances, sex frequency and styles, faith preferences and church involvement, political leanings, if you are intellectually and mentally compatible, children and families, where you want to live and vacation, and sports involvement is very important. Is he a complainer or mostly upbeat? Be sure to find out if he is conservative or liberal as this colors many other areas of a person's life from their interests to the way they live their life. Does he have a sense of humor? Does he make you laugh? Can you stay on the same page with your families, especially if you have step children or previous family connections? Be sure you both are able to have meaningful conversations and work out conflicts in a loving manner. What are your deal breakers such as sexual unfaithfulness, alcohol and drug use, lying, dishonesty, etc.? It is always best to get these issues cleared up from the very start to prevent a breakup later on.

Past hurts eventually damage or kill new relationships. Don't hesitate to get couples counseling and/or individual counseling to heal memories of old hurts and baggage. If you don't get this healed, it will be brought into new relationships and lived out over and over until it is healed. When an issue comes up, ask him if you can discuss this when you are both calm. Keep it on how it affects you and don't accuse. Remember you can learn to speak the truth in love and it will truly set you free.

Men worry about having continuing regular sex and they wonder if sex is being used to trap them into marriage. If you have any concerns about your interest in an ongoing

satisfying sexual relationship with your man, find a good
gynecologist and/or a sex counselor, get your hormone levels
checked and resolve any issues. Be able to tell your man with
total honesty that you enjoy sex and are looking forward to a
long term satisfying sexual relationship with the right man. I
guarantee you won't be without pursuers. Good men want
you to feel good sexually when you are with them. Many men
don't know how to make this happen and they really
appreciate you telling them specifically in a sexy, positive
way. Such as ..."Honey, I really love it when you touch me
this way....and show him."

There are good men out there. Like anything worth
accomplishing, the search will take time and effort. But a good
man is well worth the effort. Take your time. Beware of
anyone wanting you to pay for things. You must never give
personal or financial information to anyone you haven't met
or who has not established their credibility. A man desires
access to your heart, your life, your body and your money.
These things are very precious, hard earned and valuable.
Smart women won't give easy access to them. It is always a
losing game to use sex to try to get love. He must first
demonstrate his love and commitment over time and earn his
way into your heart.

Always remember most men are opportunistic and will take
advantage of you, if you allow it. However, many will rise to
their better selves if you sweetly and confidently require it. If
he is what you need, tell him after knowing him for six
months that you think it is time to get engaged. If a ring is not
produced within a very reasonable time, graciously say you
must move on.

NICOLA BEER

Nicola Beer is an international Relationship & Divorce Coach that helps individuals in-person and online to heal and create a new beginning. After her painful breakup, she felt totally lost when it came to being single, moving on, and dating. Through her own experience and 12 years' emotional support work, she has developed transformational programs for individuals who want to create more happiness, fun, and success in their lives. She also has a proven process for finding your soulmate.

As a child of divorce Nicola also offers parents guidance on making divorce as painless as possible for their children. She has free resources available at www.purepeacecoaching.com and a Podcast show Divorce Talk available on ITunes and Stitcher radio.

CHAPTER 7

VICTIM TO VICTOR: CREATE A NEW LIFE AFTER BREAKUP AND DIVORCE

By Nicola Beer

We see relationship breakups everywhere. Television shows dramatize steamy affairs and fragmented families, celebrity divorces are banded about on magazine covers, and politicians love tragedies make headline news, but to someone experiencing it in real time it hurts, it really hurts!

Breakups often trigger emotional chaos, mixed with confusion, and feelings of rejection and failure. Consequences that are the tip of the iceberg, as the true extent of the impact is a mass of shattered dreams, hopes and expectations.

Like a natural disaster, painful breakups have a tipping point. Where future dreams, past pain and present turmoil erupt in an emotional storm. But, like the aftermath of natural disaster, there is an opportunity to rebuild and create something new. Creating a new life takes positive energy, focus and going through a number of steps. The proven steps in the "7 R Process" take you on a journey from "Victim to Victor". Where a new you and life is manifested. You'll know you are there when you look back and say the breakup was the best thing that has ever happened to me. Not because you have gained more things, status, or even have a new relationship, (which would all be wonderful). But because you have become more of yourself, learnt to love time by yourself and know exactly how to consistently increase your own happiness and life fulfilment.

Sounds too good to be true doesn't it?

I felt like that, many do. Life can seem almost impossible when faced with the truth that your relationship didn't last long enough for your hopes and dreams to be actualized. The sense of loss can be overwhelming. During this time it can also be extremely hard to know who you can trust. Especially as advice from others comes pouring in, flooding your mind with conflicting and confusing information.

My suggestion here is simple, take a long deep breath (or several – in fact!) and accept that where you are right now, is exactly where you are meant to be. Trust yourself that YOU have the power to become a victor and follow the 7 R process below.

Honore de Balzac stated "When you doubt your power, you give power to your doubt" Don't let that happen to you, seize this opportunity to make your life great.

The 7 R Process to Creating a New Life

1 Re-energize

Energy is the foundation to creating a life you love. Rest, relaxation and learning to say no to others will go a long way. But to move out of fear, stress and feeling overwhelmed, into action and productivity you need energy.

The fastest way to get an abundance of good energy is to regularly consume nourishing fresh natural unprocessed foods (yes that means fresh fruit and vegetables) and drink plenty of water. There can be a tendency following a painful breakup to overindulge in food (often the wrong stuff, fried take outs, pizza, ice-cream and chocolate) or completely disregard it altogether. Neither aids the recovery process.

Grief and loss consumes a tremendous amount of energy, so in addition to eating healthily, you must also move your body to create more energy. It doesn't matter what physical activity you do, the important thing is you do something to reignite that spark of life inside of you.

2 Reflection

The worst advice I ever received post breakup was "Don't think about it!" It's bad advice because it is impossible to do. It is both normal and natural to review and reflect on a relationship. Reflection can be a key part to moving on if you learn from it. Don't dwell on it. Reflect only to make note of lessons learned. Use these learnings to make better choices in the future, when creating your new life. Also remain open-minded, do not judge or criticize yourself for what comes up. By reflecting upon your past only for the purpose of growth, you can create a powerful list of what you will do differently next time. Also become aware of any negative feelings you still have, so you are ready for the next step.

3 Releasing

Releasing the negative emotions inside you is the key to healing. In fact it is impossible to heal fully if you are harboring any anger, guilt, regret or sadness internally.

There are numerous ways to release these emotions, so you need to find what works best for you. Some like journaling, blogging and writing letters they never send. Others find playing out phantom conversations with their ex helps. And then there are those who invest in specialized coaching or healing to guide them to release past baggage.

Forgiveness is the key to true freedom and love. Forgiving others allows you to unlock yourself from the chains and pain of the past. Many people struggle with the concept of forgiving, because they think that it means condoning or forgetting, it means neither! Forgiveness is an action not a feeling. When people say to me they don't feel like forgiving, I reply lovingly "of course you don't, because you cannot feel something you have not done". In order to forgive you must act first, so I suggest they take the action first and then see how they feel.

There is a chance you are reading this thinking there is no way on earth I can ever forgive them, for what they said, did or put me through. I get that. Forgiveness was the hardest and most liberating thing I have ever done.

My mum suffers from mental breakdowns and during our childhood was repeatedly verbally and physically abusive. When my parents got divorced and Dad (our protector) moved away, Mum's breakdown became permanent, us 5 children had no escape from what became a progressively worse childhood. It was only when I forgave my parents wholeheartedly that I experienced true inner peace and freedom. I am not sharing my story for sympathy, or to highlight that the pain I went through was any more or less significant than yours is right now. In fact it is impossible (and therefore pointless to try) to compare our feelings with others. You know how not forgiving feels and it is your right to hold on to that if you want to. But those who hold on to it find it much harder to shift from the past.

Like many, who do take the step to forgive and accept others and their faults completely, I found I was able to love myself. By not accepting and loving my parents for who they are, warts and all, I had created an unconscious belief that: 'only people who are perfect are worthy of my love.' Therefore sending a message to myself, that I too don't deserve to be accepted and loved, as I'm not perfect either. When I forgave I could accept and love myself.

The universe often works like that, like a giant mirror projecting back what you give out or Karma, call it what you will, forgiveness works in the same way, if you forgive others you can forgive yourself. Self-forgiveness not only allows you to avoid feelings of regret, failure and self-loathing, it is necessary to move from victim to victor and create your new life.

4 Rebuilding your confidence

The breakdown of a relationship often causes your self-confidence to plummet. Self-doubt can take over your entire thought process, you begin to doubt your choices, actions, and ability to move forward. The secret to rebuilding confidence is feeling good about yourself. Taking action to boost your self-esteem may involve changes to your diet, hair style, clothes, home, career or learning something new.

Stepping out of your comfort zone can also be a great confidence builder. Going to events, parties and family gatherings as a new single can be daunting, but many find pushing through this fear is a liberating experience.

Internal work also can boost your confidence. Reminding yourself of other difficult times you've been through and survived may help you. Addressing your fears head on is also very powerful. Ask yourself "What is the worst that can happen?" and then whatever that is, list how you would cope, what actions you would take to overcome it. Attempting to ignore your fears is futile. But tackling them and reassuring yourself that you can handle it, will grow your confidence and trust in yourself.

5 Reconnecting with yourself

The relationship you have with yourself is the most important relationship you will ever have in your life. Learning to love your own company is the foundation for creating a new life on your terms.

Instead of coming home to someone else, you want to get excited about coming home to you. Imagine walking through your front door and coming home to the best version of you, fun, relaxed and happy. The you in a good mood. The you, you love spending time with, because you're only focusing on things you like to do. Whether it's surfing the net, reading, watching TV, cooking, playing video games, wine or food tasting, relaxing in the bath, DIY, gardening, indulge in activities that bring you peace and pleasure. Learning to reconnect with yourself again makes you whole. So next time as you unlock your front door, throw open your arms and welcome the playful, positive you home.

6 Recruit a support team

While it is important to strengthen your self-trust and self-love muscles, it is just as important to get the help you need from others. Breakups and divorce can leave you reeling for support but unsure of where to get it. Not all friends and family may be good for you, so take control and recruit a team of people that makes you feel strong. A team that doesn't allow you to wallow in your pain but encourages you to move forward and be the best you can be.

7 Rediscovering your true values

After years of looking after other's needs, many find they have lost themselves in their relationship. One lady I worked with compared leaving her marriage after 20 years, to leaving home at 18. Most breakups can lead you to question who you are, what you want and what will make you happy.

The easiest way to create a life that will bring you lasting happiness and fulfilment is to rediscover and live by your values. To rediscover your values you must ask yourself "What is really important to me to have in my life now and in the future?" Asking yourself this question several times over (or better still get a friend to ask you) will give you some guiding principles to live, plan and make life decisions by.

The 7 R Process has been proven to get outstanding results for those who are fully committed to create a new life for themselves. In the journey from victim to victor, positive energy and making room for a new life are essential to manifesting it.

Here are my 2 secret tips to help you along with the 7 R process to manifest your dream life.

ADDITIONAL MANIFESTING TIPS

Tip 1 - MAKE ROOM FOR YOUR NEW LIFE
In order to manifest a new life you need to declutter and make room for the new you to flourish. Just like new plants need the weeds to be cleared for them to grow, so you need to eliminate weeds. Clear out your closets, cupboards, and refrigerator and dump any old bed linen. All the while affirming that you are clearing out the old from your mind and life and making room for the new. Enjoy it! It is meant to feel good as you say goodbye victim hello victor.

Tip 2 - KEEP POSITIVE ENERGY FLOWING

It is widely accepted that staying positive, being grateful and looking forward to the future, has the power to create more good in our lives. But doing that is not always easy. In fact sometimes it can seem almost impossible to shift a bad mood.

Use music to get you feeling great again and give the manifestation process a super boost.

Manifesting a New Life

Let the good vibrations guide you towards the life you deserve. Here are some suggestions:

For Positive Energy and to Embrace Your New Future:
"What a Wonderful Life" Elvis Presley
"I can see clearly now" Johnny Nash
"Feeling Good" (I put a spell on you) Nina Simone
"Grace and Gratitude" Olivia-Newton John
"Best day of my life" American Authors
"Happy" Pharrell Williams
"Brand New Sun" Beck
"Sun is Shining" Bob Marley

To forgive yourself and overcome guilt
"Sweet Streams" Kirtana

To love yourself
"The Greatest Love of All" Whitney Houston

KAREN WILTSHIRE

Karen Wiltshire is a Transition/Life Coach. She uses her intuitive sense, wisdom and knowledge to help others transition from one stage of life to the next. Whether it is a loss of a loved one, separation or divorce, Karen brings courage and conviction to her clients.

"Grief never ends...but it changes. It's a passage, not a place to stay. Grief is not a sign of weakness, nor a lack of faith...It is the price for love,'

Facebook: https://www.facebook.com/karen.wiltshire.71
LinkedIn: https://www.linkedin.com/pub/karen-wiltshire/1b/10a/453
Website: www.googlecom/YourPeaceofPower
Email: kebwiltshire@hotmail.com

CHAPTER 8

THE BENCH

By Karen Wiltshire

THE BENCH

Our memories are etched in the bench, which holds the untold stories of our existence. Sitting on the bench allows so many to go to the secret place in their hearts. The bench has a great purpose, therefore....in my opinion has a soul.

Our lives can be altered by unforeseen events, like a sudden downpour in the middle of a picnic.

In some ways it can be a gift, even though sometimes it does not feel that way. I did not recognize this until much later. Back then to say my heart was broken cannot express the depth of my pain.

With the sudden end of my twenty-three year marriage, it was more like my heart had third degree burns. It was the rawest of feelings. My days and nights were long and filled with anxiety and despair. I felt as if I was made of broken glass. At times I was afraid to breathe as I imagined shattering into a million pieces it was as if I was in deep treacherous waters. The waves kept thrashing at me and whenever I felt safe and could take a breath, another wave would slam me, pushing me deeper and deeper to the bottom. My body expressed the twisted guts of the situation. I was diagnosed with Crohn's disease. Being hospitalized for an attack was an emotional vacation, as the morphine administered to me helped me to escape my reality.

In desperation I went to spiritual healers, hypnotists, psychics and doctors to see if they could give me medication for my heart. More often than not, I would lie on the couch until my girls came home from school. My friend Kelly, would take my dog during the day, as I could not care for him. My sisters would take me to my appointments, as I could not drive. It took me at least two years to be able to listen to music as I had so much noise in my mind. Sometimes I prayed to be taken.

I am a very spiritual person but then I began to realize that the way I prayed was not working. Looking back when I was so full of fear, my prayers were destructive and desperate. I was sending myself into an emotional tailspin. When I did not see the changes I was begging for, my frustration deepened. God where are you? Don't you see me? I felt so depleted.

Throughout my life I have always been fascinated with benches. I know that the bench has been as important to me as it is a place that I can reflect on my journey thus far as well a place to stay put to make decision for forward movements in my life. It just feels safe to me. I wonder who

has sat there before me and who will sit there after me. Sitting on the bench is always enriching for me whether it is physical or in my mind's eye. It is my portal to a more peaceful and purposeful life and has allowed me to make true insights.

85

Manifesting a New Life

It was also my time on the bench that allowed me to reclaim my life. I recall lying on a bench in a park, crying uncontrollably. A stranger called the police to say there was a woman in distress. This was a turning point for me as I knew that I was not going to let my situation sink me. My girls needed me.

I realized I was not alone. I had my earthly angels, my family, friends, and my beautiful girls. I also had another special person in my life, my therapist Michelle.
Every Tuesday and Thursday, she provided me with the wisdom needed to just make it through the day. She then went on to help me developed the skills needed to ride the wave that often threatened to envelope me. With the work Michelle and I did together I have been able to go on with hope for joy and love.

This is not an easy process with every step forward, there were doubts and despair. I can reflect on the way I reacted to my situation. With hard work and my new found wisdom, I realized that I had a choice about the way I responded to things around me. I had put myself into this state and it was up to me to get myself out of it.

In addition to therapy, breaking my pattern of prayer was one of the most beneficial acts I did to launch myself forward. It was also one of my greatest feats. I was so angry with God, instead of trusting him, begging to have my old life back. Yet a slow powerful transformation began to take place deep inside of me. In time, my frustration began to dissipate and I began to understand that the restoration of the soul can only come about when one is willing to break one's destructive patterns. When I began to trust in myself and in God, I knew spiritually I was growing.

I also had to let go to move forward, even when I did not want to. To value and be grateful for our past and thank those who were a part of it, is a great act of kindness. Wishing form the heart that those we love or loved to find true joy and peace is liberating. Being grateful for love and pain, is what pushes us forward emotionally and spiritually.

Whatever destination we choose I know that it must be chosen with passion, for passion is enlightenment. Being enlightened guides us to a more peaceful and purposeful existence. As well, I learned that forgives is love. We must love ourselves before we love others and we must forgive ourselves before we can forgive others. When we can own our own human mishaps, and not blame others for our decisions is a huge step in emotional maturity. There is no value in beating others into the ground.

With this emotional and spiritual awakening, I now had to figure out how to live my new life. After gratefully being home with my girls a new found career was essential. My first question to myself was what do I love in this life? The answer came quickly; People, I love people. A friend of mine suggested I look into becoming a Life Coach. At this point, still emotionally fragile, my enrollment for certification was via tele class. Twelve people from all over the world met weekly on the telephone with an instructor. Week to week my passion for coaching grew. My inner self was awakening with each conference call and assignment.

We all walk through darkness at some point in our lives. To

Manifesting a New Life

take someone's hand so to speak, walk with them, to help them see their light is precious. This period of time in my life offers great exploration and growth. The way I can help someone, help themselves puts a stamp on my life. Guiding others by remembering the lessons learned from my responses when faced with adversity has made me pay attention to my own emotional intelligence .Coaching continues to push me forward. It is a great step towards optimism and deepens my belief that everyone has their own unique purpose.

My shadows are still with me at times, but it is clear to me that pain is essential for growth and therefor has a purpose. Drawing on my deep spiritual beliefs, the love of family and friends, the countless hours of therapy and prayer, I have found the hope to move forward. My hope becomes determination and obstacles become possibilities. Confidence and conviction have returned slowly. My inner strength is an instrument I have learned to call upon.

The goal for my life is to touch as many people as I can in a positive way. To have courage and be kind I now begin my day with prayer that is not self-centered but rather one of reflection, filled with family and friends and those in need. Through this process my character has flourished and my faith has been restored.

In the past I have viewed myself as one dimensional and in black and white. Today, understanding my natural gifts, I know I am very much in color. My broken marriage, although filled with pain, also provided me with the greatest gift. I am so blessed to be the mother of my wonderful daughters, Kathryn and Meghan.

As I look back, I want to hug my broken self and exalt in the fact that not only did I survive, but today I am helping others do the same.

"Grief never ends...but it changes. It's a passage, not a place to stay. Grief is not a sign of weakness or lack of faith...it is the price for love".

A TREASURED MESSAGE FROM MY GIRLS

"We hope that one day we can be as courageous, caring, kind and selfless as our mom. We watched her go through the hardest ten years of her life, while rising two teenage daughters going through issues of our own.

She always put us first, making sure we were happy and taken care of. In a heartbeat our mom would sacrifice her own happiness for her children, her family and friends, even complete strangers. In our opinion, the depth of her empathy is a very rare thing in this world. She is the strongest woman we know and is not only an amazing role model but also our best friend. She is truly an inspirational human being. We have learned so many life lessons from her, but also have witnessed her blossom into a strong independent woman. We are so happy to see her rebuild herself and the life she deserves as she has worked so hard to do. With this chapter, to see our mom share her story and the wisdom she has gained, will no doubt help others.

Our mom is the perfect example of the proverb: What doesn't kill you makes you stronger.

Manifesting a New Life

We love you mom. Thank you for making this world a better place xoxoxo

DR. JOE PRATILE, DC, BKIN (HONS)

Dr. Joe Pratile is a Doctor of Chiropractic Medicine, Director of Health and owner of the Toronto Muscle Doctor. A debilitating back injury and the ensuing success of his treatments opened his eyes to chiropractic care and the importance of balancing the brain to heal the body. This revelation led to a career in chiropractic medicine, where he is passionate about using multi-sensory conditioning, meditation and relaxation strategies that go beyond touch therapy. His practice focuses on helping his patients achieve optimal overall wellness through a full understanding and harmonization of the brain and the body.

Email: DrJoePratile@gmail.com
Phone: 647-654-5639
Location: Toronto, Ontario, Canada
Time Zone: EST
Facebook FanPage: https://www.facebook.com/pages/Dr-Joe-Pratile/1460400754228752
Facebook Personal
Page: https://www.facebook.com/joey.pratile.9
Twitter: https://twitter.com/drjoepratile
LinkedIn: https://ca.linkedin.com/pub/dr-joe-pratile/31/529/402
Instagram: https://instagram.com/drjoepratile/

CHAPTER 9

HOW TO HAVE SEX WITH YOUR BRAIN

By Dr. Joe Pratile, DC, BKIN (HONS)

As a kid, I was extremely disruptive in school. I was smart, I got great marks, but I misbehaved badly. I had undiagnosed Attention Deficit Disorder (ADD) because my father refused to get me tested. He was worried that the ensuing stigma would threaten my academic standing. I remember being told ADD was a gift that was just difficult to unwrap. I felt like I had a Ferrari mind, but with bicycle brakes.

Sports and exercise helped me cope with my disorder. I didn't fully realize how much it balanced me out until I suffered a debilitating disc herniation in my lower back. I quickly learned how chiropractic medicine could heal both my body and my mind. Not only did it help my back, it also completely de-stressed my brain and rewired my nervous system and physiology. I was soon able to adapt, respond, and recover to experiences that previously set off my ADD on a higher level than ever before.

As a practitioner now, I have seen time and time again how relaxation predicates realization. Experience has taught me that when you balance and relax the brain, the body will always follow. So, how can you have sex with your brain?

There are four basic human needs for both brain expansion and sexual happiness: consistency, variety, significance or uniqueness of experience, and love and/or connection to a social support network. We all want consistency in our partners and our brains want that, too—nerves that fire together, wire together. At the same time, uncertainty is equally important; challenging yourself with novel experiences is a prerequisite to growth and change, both in the bedroom and the brain. Significance of experience stems from each individual's unique lens of perception; our perspectives are personal, special, and should be coveted. Finally, love and social support is fundamental to humanity. It creates a space that allows for vulnerability where you can let go of the past in order to propel yourself forward.

Mastery of these four basic needs will ultimately lead to higher growth and contribution. Without knowledge, practice, and self-awareness, you will not be able to nourish and stimulate yourself effectively enough to keep you happy, satisfied, and having that overall feel-good feeling that comes with proper health.

One important concept I have come to adopt in treating my clients is multisensory conditioning. Touch, sight, smell, hearing, vibration, even taste—they all trigger various brain functions and can be influenced in ways that will balance the brain to renew the body.

The first step in brain balancing is to detect your brain dominance pattern. In my practice, I assess my clients with Dr. Robert Melillo's master hemispheric checklist to discover left/right brain dominance patterns. Once each person's unique pattern is understood, we can begin to work on balance.

Two especially powerful methods are smell and sound therapy. For example, those with left brain dominance can stimulate the right brain by inhaling certain scents or essential oils through the right nostril while keeping the left one covered. Right brain stimulators include black pepper, burnt wood, coffee, eucalyptus, fish oil, lemon, lime, mustard, onion, and peppermint. Conversely, right brain dominance can be trained with such left brain stimulators as apple, banana, cherry, chocolate, grape, lavender, orange, pineapple, rose, and strawberry.

To train the brain with sound therapy, block the ear of your dominant side with an earplug and listen with the opposite ear. Right brain music includes low frequency, harmony-based, long-term pattern selections such as Mozart's Piano Concerto No. 26 and Schubert's March Militaire. Left brain music includes higher frequency stimuli that carry more detailed information, often with lyrics and rapid variance in volume, rhythm, timing, and pitch, such as Bach's Air on a G String or Tchaikovsky's Piano Concerto in B Minor.

Mindfit light/sound meditation is another fun brain balancing tool. I call it "meditation on steroids" because you can achieve profound relaxation in just 10--20 minutes. It uses calming blue lights pulsing at specific frequencies to guide visualization, while relaxing tones play on a headset. Dr. Rodger K. Cady and Dr. Norman Shealy found that this type of self-mastery technology increases Beta-endorphins (which decrease pain) by 25%, Serotonin (which enhances social pride) by 21%, and Norepinephrine (which increases euphoria) by 11%. Furthermore, dynamic EEG testing has proved that this kind of meditation activates neuroplasticity, thereby balancing out your brainwaves to leave your brain harmonized and recharged.

These conscious states of relaxed control maximize sensory integration, resulting in brain balance, growth, and expansion. Increasing the amount of sensory information for the brain to process stimulates its renewal. This is where variety and uniqueness of experience comes into play; challenging your mind to dynamically respond to cues allows it to expand itself beyond familiar limitations. You are brought closer to your true self by a renewal of your own reality within a state of total freedom.

Margaret Thatcher once said, "If you want anything said, ask a man. If you want anything done, ask a woman." Of course, we can't talk about sex without talking about the differences between male and female brains.

On the chromosomal level, females are XX and males are XY. At the cerebral level, male brains are 8-10% larger with about 4% more neurons. They also have a larger amygdala, the brain center that processes fear and anger, which explains why men in crises often jump to those emotions. Men tend to be more left brain dominant—they see the trees and neglect the forest. The left brain is more analytical, logical, detail-oriented, and stronger at executing plans.

The unique Y chromosome carries the instructions for the male testicles to produce large amounts of testosterone halfway through pregnancy, differentiating between male and female. Astonishingly, psychologist Simon Baron-Cohen found in the Cambridge Longitudinal Fetal Testosterone (FT) Project that as fetal testosterone levels increase, empathy, eye contact, and intuition decrease.

Women exhibit an infinitely higher capacity for emotional responses, language, judgment, planning and collaboration, impulse control, empathy, and conscientiousness. This is because in comparison to men, women have larger volume frontal and limbic cortices, which are responsible for higher cognitive functions and emotional responsiveness.

Women tend to use more of the right brain, which is the home of creativity. It sees the bigger picture and is responsible for patterns, hunches, and intuition. It draws upon connections and neuro associations to more distant parts of the brain and uses a higher quantity of different inputs to reach conclusions. Brain imaging also consistently shows that the major memory centers in the brain, the hippocampus, is larger in women.

An optimally healthy brain can maximize its ability to adapt, respond, and recover from stress by striking a balance between these two personalities; it works in concert to share and collaborate information across nerve bundles. Today, most men and an increasing number of women are becoming left brain dominant. For many, right brain intuition is hard to accept and often dismissed as emotional, unreasonable and unscientific.

Albert Einstein understood it best when he stated, "The intuitive mind is a sacred gift and the rational mind a faithful servant." We have created a society that honors the servant while forgetting the gift. It's most important to know yourself and your dominance tendencies so that you can train your brain to make decisions with both sides. Amassing this personal knowledge of your unique functional neurology will allow you to prepare your brain for the healthiest, happiest, most fruitful life possible.

Our brains are paths to pleasure and the connection between the brain and the body is undeniable — you can't have one without the other. As much as sex (and all the pleasures that come with it) is an act of the body, the brain is equally important. You will not experience pleasure if you are stressed. In everything from spa treatments to healing exercises to reaching climax, the first step is to relax. Only then will you be able to tune into yourself to piece together the various mental and physical processes that are occurring within you. Only then will you be able to maximize your potential for stimulation, nourishment, excitement, self-healing, and happiness.

At only 2-3% of our body weight, the human brain is our most powerful organ, consuming roughly 20-30% of our daily caloric intake. It's the most complex and expensive piece of real estate we own and with that complexity comes potential. But often, people will settle for accepting their brain in its current state, unaware of the work that can be done to improve its strength and functionality. We accept that we are as smart or as happy as we are (or are not). But why settle? Why not unlock your potential and tap into your power?

Do you feel confident in your natural ability to balance your energy, mood, relaxation, power, trust, and lust? Are you ready to fall in love with your brain, to start loving it and treating it right? First seek balance, and the rest will follow.

Manifesting a New Life

ROXIE DE ANGELIS CHEF, RNC, RHC

Nutrition = (Food + Passion + Nostalgia) Ritual

I introduce this equation to every client and in each class I teach. Food can be life changing and changing your life is my passion.

Before I became a Holistic Practitioner, I studied aromatherapy spa, colonics, Reiki and ear candling. Among other programs, I graduated from the Canadian School of Natural Nutrition in Holistic Nutrition and became certified at the Chef Training Program and Basic Health Supportive Cooking at the Natural Gourmet Cookery School in NYC.

Cooking can be extremely spiritual and it is invariably an extension of my soul. With that said, I wish to share this experience with you.

Website: chiliandfennel.com

Facebook & Instagram: @chilifennelculinary

CHAPTER 10

NUTRITION = RITUAL

By Roxie De Angelis Chef, RNC, RHC

Imagine this:

You take out a pan and gently place it on the range while setting the heat dial to medium. You then add a touch of oil, no more than a tablespoon. As the oil begins to sizzle, you add one sliced pear. The following ingredients that come to mind are fennel seeds and a few slices of local grown peaches. Can you smell it? Can you envision it? Can you hear the sound of the sizzling pan as the tantalizing aroma emanating from the pan starts to fill the room? Sautee all of it and then lay it over a bed of wilted spinach. Finish it off with sprinkles of lavender. Have a seat and take a moment to fully enjoy the beautiful dish you've just created.

Okay, so you're probably wondering…what was all that about?

Not only was this a premeditated healthy breakfast that included organic and local ingredients, but it was a ritual; my breakfast ritual. Just the word "ritual" brings back so many memories. It takes me back to days when I used to own my Bed and Breakfast in Toronto. Every morning I would cater to my guests with vegan or vegetarian and gluten-free meals. The process of making these breakfasts was meditative and somewhat spiritual.

When I think of food and cooking, this equation comes to mind.
Nutrition = (Food + Passion + Nostalgia) Ritual

When I studied nutrition, I always felt like it involved more than just the food. I came to realize that passion and nostalgia combined with food created ritual. Which in turn, is the true definition of nutrition. Later in life, I've come to understand that I'm living proof of the above equation.

So who am I?

My given name at birth was Rossana De Angelis, but I go by Roxie (mostly because it's easier for people to pronounce). I'm first generation Italian-Canadian and as a person of Italian decent, my love affair with food essentially started at birth. However, there was one problem. I was also born with severe IBS (irritable bowel syndrome), which later included an unbearable intolerance to gluten as well. As I got older and began to become more aware of my condition, I became obsessed with food.

Food

Growing up with IBS wasn't easy.

My first memory of food was when I was 6 years old making gnocchi with my sister. We never went to summer camp, instead, my sister and I would take handfuls of dough and make gnocchi for hours, to feed family members who quite often showed up unexpectedly at our house. That's how I remember my childhood. It consisted of incredibly delicious home-cooked meals that we always shared with amazing company.

As I got older, I continued to eat the same foods as my family, however I subsequently became sicker every year. This was when my obsession for wellness intensified. "How is it that I'm eating the same as everyone else and feeling worse?" I constantly thought to myself.

As a child, I was always sick and would have terrible IBS attacks on a consistent basis. I was very confused as to why this was happening and couldn't figure out the cause. My condition worsened when my family and I moved to the suburbs of Toronto. Family gatherings lessened and daily family dinners at 6:00pm were replaced with dinner at my grandparents or sitting alone in front of the TV. And then just as suddenly, another shift happened. When I became a teenager, I was allowed to work and with that I could no longer participate in Sunday family lunches and dinners. Consequently, my IBS became even more horrendous.

I never put two and two together when it came to the ritual of eating together and my well-being. My condition caused me a lot of pain during school and resulted in missing lots of classes and cancelling work. At this point, my frustration had reached its peak and I decided to pursue the study of Holistic Nutrition.

Passion

I craved answers, but I always felt I was still lacking information. In my early twenties, I studied holistic nutrition, colon hydrotherapy, aroma-spa and learned about medicinal herbs, even ear candling. One course led to another and yet another, but I still wasn't finding the answers I needed. I went to culinary school hoping to learn how to use medicinal herbs and foods to aid in healthy nutrition, but traditional French cooking was still on the course curriculum at the time and holistic nutrition wasn't popular enough to be taught in conventional cooking schools. Exasperated, I gave up and went into banking.

You're probably thinking "banking? Why the heck would you do that?"

Despite this sudden switch in careers, it was in fact the best decision I had ever made because that's when I became the sickest I had ever been.

I am a workaholic by nature and as such I put all of my energy into banking; which meant long hours, bringing work home, completely ditching my social life and never eating on time. Upon reaching my second anniversary of working at the bank, inevitably, my worst nightmare returned; my IBS. Incidentally, I was always told I was a nervous child and that was the reason as to why I experienced stomach cramps. It never occurred to me that the gastrointestinal pain was in fact a result of being without my family and eating alone. I do have a tendency to be emotional, sometimes a bit too emotional, and that added to the severity of my IBS; but I didn't think those two correlated.

Manifesting a New Life

Stress, loneliness, bad eating times and habits were the nails in my coffin. Out of desperation, I pleaded with my doctor to find a solution to these reoccurring problems I regularly experienced. As a child and teenager, I missed too many days from school, and now, my health was threatening my status at work. I felt completely helpless. After years of being told I had lazy bowels and a nervous stomach, I was finally diagnosed with IBS at the age of 25. "Finally" I thought "A name to my condition". They gave me some pills I thought were magic because I believed they were the answer to my decades of pain. However, to my utter dismay, those pills were a curse. After taking 3 types of medication, I was forced to take sick leave.

While on sick leave, I realized I needed to get back into nutrition and cooking for the sake of my health. I stumbled upon a school in New York City that combined my love for nutrition with the culinary arts… it was perfect!! With my vacation time, I took a two-week intensive course, which later led to taking courses every weekend and I travelled back and forth from Toronto to NYC on my days off. My parents began to notice a difference in my overall well-being and we agreed that this school was the best thing for me and would certainly aid in my recovery.

Before we go any further, I would like to reference some case studies that reinforce my equation. One of them is the "The Roseto Effect"[1] a study of a close-knit Italian-American community in Roseto, Pennsylvania around the 1960's. In a

---

[1] Link found here
http://www.uic.edu/classes/osci/osci590/14_2%20The%20Roseto%20Effect.htm

nutshell, the citizens of Roseto lived their lives in a community that truly was a community. Despite their bad habits, their health wasn't compromised due to low stress yet there remained constant community support within the town. However, when the second and third generations of Roseto grew up, their health wasn't nearly as good as that of their parents or grandparents. This was all because the close-knit culture of community support, love and even the simple act of eating together dissipated, which caused a chain reaction of poor health.

The second study I'd like to reference is from "The Blue Zones"[2]. This study looks at three different parts of the world where it's common to live past 100 years old. The prevalent commonalities in key life components these areas shared were essentially: eating well, exercise, spirituality and community gathering. The older generations spent time with the younger ones and there was an extreme level of respect between people. Discrimination was never present and everyone always wanted to help one another.

To return, in New York City I proceeded to take the holistic culinary course. My diet was extremely healthy, but I still managed to become very sick because I didn't have my friends or family to support me, or even eat with me! I was missing this very important ritual in my life. But as soon as I made friends, cooked with them and began practicing yoga, my IBS virtually disappeared and in addition, I released 30lbs of physical weight and my emotional stress vanished.

---

[2] Link Found here
http://www.bluezones.com/wp-content/uploads/2011/02/Nat_Geo_Longevity.pdf

Manifesting a New Life

Every now and then, I gain some weight because being a chef isn't the easiest lifestyle. The days are long and the breaks are short, but when I do get a quick 15 minutes in my shift, I always try to mediate, walk or stretch. Despite the long hours and crazy lifestyle, being a chef taught me how to better communicate with food. This in turn, made me a better nutritionist because it gave me the tools and understanding as to how to better cater to someone's specific nutritional needs. What I love most about my job, and similarly what keeps me sane, is finishing a dinner service and then meeting with friends to cook, eat and enjoy each other's company.

Nostalgia
I also had two very memorable experiences throughout my travels: one was a trip to Italy and the other to Argentina. When I was in Italy, I was working as a liaison for a cooking school for Canada. Every morning, I would meet with the administration staff in the office for our daily ritual of espresso, gossip and they would always ask me what my dinner plans were. "Dinner?" I thought, "I just had breakfast!" I later learned that when you're in Italy and someone asks you "what's for dinner? "It's a fully loaded question. It entails what you're eating, where you're going, whom you'll be with and what the after dinner plans are.

At the cooking school, the chefs and students prepped and cooked for four hours, which was followed by a two-hour break where we enjoyed the food we created over wine and conversation. We weren't simply digesting the food, but the entire experience. When I was asked the dinner question again, I finally understood how to respond to this cryptic inquiry over espresso and gossip. It became a daily ritual!

When I took my trip to Argentina, it was purely for soul searching purposes. At the time, I was forced to close my bed and breakfast in the city because the transit company needed my property in order to expand a subway line. I felt like I was losing everything; my home, my business, my life's work. I had put so much love and care into my B&B and felt as though it was an end to my career as a chef and hostess. I left Toronto feeling very lost. But when I got to Argentina, I somehow learned how to live again!

In Argentina, the lifestyle is very different than that of North Americans. People wake up between 6:00am-7:00am for work and end their day around 6:00pm. They take a nap after work and as soon as they wake up, they eat dinner out with their friends or go to a club and then come home. They do this 7 days a week. This was all completely foreign to me, however I embraced it whole-heartedly. The intoxicating smells of all the foods, the laughter people shared over a meal and of course, all of the wonderful company really made my trip memorable and somehow in the process I was able to rediscover myself. It was indeed the perfect trip. I came back to Toronto completely recharged and I promised myself that even on a busy night after work, I would always make time to spend reconnecting with people.

All these life experiences taught me that true nutrition is this simple equation.

And that, dear readers, is the way we maintain true wellness.

Nutrition = (Food + Passion + Nostalgia) Ritual

Thank you, Roxie De Angelis

Manifesting a New Life

Samantha Richardson

Samantha Richardson is a writing coach and editor. She has been writing creatively for over 15 years, building her writing and editing skills. As a coach, Samantha finds great joy in helping others find their voice and overcome writers block, as she supports them to improve their writing skills so they can share their stories and wisdom with the world.

Samantha coaches one-on-one (in-person or online) and in small group retreats to help those needing extra support to write their book and connect others with their inner muse.

To read more about Samantha and her work, go to www.lovinghearteditor.com.

Chapter 11

My Journey in Healing from Depression

By Samantha Richardson

Right now I am fully committed to living my dream life. I am claiming my worth as a writer, who can help others overcome their writing blocks, and dedicating my life to the profession. The validation I felt the first time I was paid for my writing and editing skills moved me to tears, because my childhood dream of being a writer was finally becoming reality.

However, it wasn't always this way. I've suffered from crippling depression for most of my life. I won't lie; recovering from the deep self-hatred that causes depression isn't easy. It is a constant battle between the relentless barrage of self-hatred and self-doubt, and tentative hope that I am healing.

Recently, I experienced a bout of depression that completely floored me. I was not prepared for the level of despair and anguish I felt. When this downward spiral was triggered, I began to question the wisdom of following my dreams. And on the worst days, when my depression was an all-consuming black hole of misery - I was ready to give up. On those days, I couldn't see anything but the lack of money in my bank account, and the extreme exhaustion from my seemingly inconsequential efforts. That's when I came close to turning away from my dream, because it was too big. I had to defy so many expectations to make the dream work. And I could not bear the weight of it when also faced with the monster that is my depression.

Depression is the killer of dreams.

In the depths of depression - you are in a 'vicious cycle'. It is the constant downwards spiral that leads to bottomless, uninterrupted pits of self-hatred. It matters where you put your attention - if you are in a Cycle of Hate, the only way out of it is to construct a Cycle of Love. It may be too difficult at first to declare love for yourself, and all the wonderful pieces of who you are - so start with something small. Start with something you can believe in. For instance, I love the way my friends come to my aid whenever I need them.

I remember a specific moment where I was wallowing in self-pity and self-hating thoughts - when I had an epiphany. My self-talk was not true; it had no basis in reality other than what I created inside my head. If I was creating a reality where I was unloved, useless, and stupid - couldn't I create a reality where I was as successful, brilliant, and loved as I wanted to be? Once I had come to this realization, I began to shape my external world to one that served me. I began searching for stories that filled me with hope, rather than despair.

Focusing on the amazing success stories from people who are making the world a better place, was my first choice in creating a Cycle of Love. I was so amazed at how this created an outlook of hope for life - that despite something I had previously considered 'a hopeless case', there was someone out there proving me wrong and creating solutions. It fueled me with a desire to become one of those people. I wanted to create Cycles of Love for everyone whom I touch with my stories. To do this, I knew I had to create my own Cycle of Love.

My first step in recovery was to begin focusing my energy on things that were easy to change. I began meditating regularly. I went to therapy and joined online courses and groups that were exceptionally self-empowering. Writing is the most important thing in my life, so I joined a writing group I connected with, and encouraged myself to be more creative. I also took a job that provided me with routine, and validation of my abilities so I could begin rebuilding my self-worth.

At the time, I couldn't believe it possible to be a full-time writer, so I stayed in that job. While it wasn't yet my ideal life, it was a critical step in my recovery. Without it, I would not have been able to restore my courage enough to take the leap of faith to pursue a writing career when the opportunity presented itself.

The next critical step in my recovery was learning to ask for help. The one thing I was adamant about during this period of time was refusing to put up the mask of "I'm fine," when I very clearly wasn't. So when people would ask how I was doing, I would tell them, "I'm actually not doing so great, I've been having a hard time lately." Then I could chose to share, and it opened the door for others to help me. Letting my friends and loved ones know that I was having a rough time allowed them to extend a hand of support. I just had to take it. I couldn't take care of myself in those moments, and I had to learn to let others take care of me.

Unlearning the Cycle of Hate is a multi-layered process that takes years. It is the process of rewriting the story of how you live your life. One of the biggest struggles is maintaining a positive, optimistic mindset. When things start to go wrong, especially when money doesn't show up when you need it to, it can set off a chain reaction that can suck you into a black hole of fear, doubt and tears. In those moments, you have to learn to be fiercely compassionate with yourself. Then, act fast. Do whatever it takes to stabilize your emotions, which usually involves receiving support from loved ones, because the encouragement of self-care helps speed up your recovery time.

I used to feel pathetic for saying I needed help, so I would bury the need further, until it began eating me alive. But I realized if I wanted to manifest my dream life, I had to say "yes" to receiving help *especially* in the dark times. Because that's when I needed the most help. The worst part of depression is suffering in silence. But when I would bring myself to extend my hand to ask for help, I would constantly be surprised by just how much people were willing to help. This support allowed me to see the love that was all around me, and it always had been.

As soon as I acknowledged this love, took care of myself, focused on my support, my meditation and my goals - within a very short period of time, money showed up. I was being rewarded for taking care of myself, and not allowing myself to be overwhelmed into a scarcity mindset. Obviously, I cannot always maintain a positive mindset (I don't think there's a person alive who doesn't sometimes experience doubt), but the real tests and rewards come from choosing abundance and faith again, and again, and <u>again</u>.

Once I had built up my internal strength, I was ready to face my fears and step out of my comfort zone. After I began to do this, I realized that fear is the only thing that shrinks as you embrace it. It no longer has a paralyzing hold over you. Whereas when I embrace love and gratitude, I feel myself expand and open up to more love. Knowing this, I just have to be brave enough to face each new fear as they arise, so they shatter and I emerge reborn as a healthier, happier person.

This is a life-long process that reveals itself as we discover new sources of pain, and dig deeper into old wounds. I know will get through it, because I have survived much worse. That knowing burns like a beacon of hope shining through the darkness of depression, while I claw my way back into the light of love.

Now that I'm open to receiving the gift of life, surrounded by the people I want to emulate, things fall out of the universe, just waiting for me to say 'yes' to receiving them. They were always there, but in my depressive state, I could not see them. I was not encouraged to follow my passion as a writer by my family, only to consider it a hobby. It was impossible for me to do this though. I needed to be creative to feed my soul, so I refused to stop pursuing my dream of becoming a published author. And one day I saw clearly the choice I had: continuing what I've always been doing, or taking that leap of faith and finally pursuing being a writer. That's when I decided I had to follow my heart, and live my true passion. I may have lucked out in some respects, but luck is what happens when persistence and preparedness meets opportunity.

ELENA CHEREMET

If you want to improve your health and your chances of staying away from cancer, you need to hear about the Natural Health program Elena Cheremet developed. A cancer survivor, she researched alternative remedies, declined chemo and radiotherapy and became cancer-free by changing her diet and lifestyle. She is an acclaimed author, public speaker, blogger, professional life coach, and energy healing enthusiast on a mission to educate people about the power of nutrition. Leverage Elena's experience of cancer-free living and learn how to get in touch with the body's inner healing forces and improve your health naturally.

Website/ blog: http://www.wordsofhealth.com/

Facebook: https://www.facebook.com/wordsofhealth

Pinterest (recipes):
https://www.pinterest.com/elenacheremet/healthy-food-recipes/

Linked-In: https://ca.linkedin.com/pub/elena-cheremet/102/335/537

CHAPTER 12

CANCER-FREE WITH NUTRITION: MY JOURNEY OF NATURAL HEALTH.

By Elena Cheremet

"Let food be thy medicine and medicine be thy food."
— Hippocrates, 4th century BC

I don't know why people get cancer.
It can happen to anyone, at any age. I don't know why.
Cancer attacks the young and the old, the healthy and the sick.
I don't know why.
I don't know what happened when cancer took my mother, at the age of 59, in just three short agonizing months.
I don't know why my grandfather lost his cancer battle many years ago.
I don't know why I got it when I was only 37.

What I do know is that every single cell in our body has a built-in mechanism of self-repair and self-healing. Our body has an option of activating this mechanism at any given moment. Within this amazingly strong and capable, but also very fragile physical body, every single person has the hidden power to stop cancer and live a long happy healthy life.

My cancer diagnosis came out of the blue in the fall of 2007. I was living a happy life filled with love, fun and creativity. A great loving husband, two beautiful daughters, a flourishing career and fantastic friends – I had it all. Life was well-balanced and nothing could go wrong. Until one day, after a couple of painful tests, my doctor sat down with me in her office and told me that the little pea-sized lump in my left breast was actually cancer.

What do most people do when facing a life-threatening condition? Overwhelmed with fear, they rely upon the health professionals, giving up the control and responsibility for their own well-being and survival. In many cases this *is* the best thing to do. Doctors do save lives on a daily basis, they do know how to fix a lot of issues a human body might be struggling with.

In the case of cancer, however, the situation is different. Modern medicine does not have all the answers. It is treating many cancers with the same type of aggressive treatment. Indeed, cancer therapy needs to be very aggressive: destroying the stubborn, ever-multiplying cancer cells is no easy task. Only strong medication can do the job. Unfortunately, normal healthy cells get destroyed in the process as well. Chemotherapy kills cancer but it also kills the immune system leaving the person susceptible to many adverse conditions including cancer relapse.

"We are offering you the best treatment we have" – my oncologist told me when I decided to decline the therapy. And it's true: radio and chemotherapy *is* the best treatment the modern medicine has to offer, nothing else is available. Our advanced, sophisticated, life-saving medicine can do a lot of things. It cannot, however, do the body's work for it.

Manifesting a New Life

Cell mutation occurs much more often than we would care to admit. A strong healthy immune system recognizes the "intruders" and destroys them. But sometimes, things go wrong, the mutated cells start playing hide-and-seek, and the immune system fails to "see" them. And a tumor begins to grow.

I believe in addressing health issues at the root. Our immune system is equipped with everything that's needed to keep cancer and many other diseases at bay. And if the immune system fails, wouldn't it be logical to try and make it stronger so that it could deal with whatever went wrong in the first place?

This is what I thought when I regained the ability to think clearly. My surgery that removed the cancerous lump, shortly before Christmas and several weeks past the initial diagnosis, went well. The pathology results were coming after the holidays, and I was scheduled to undergo chemotherapy followed by radiation therapy. Meanwhile, I started to slowly emerge out of the fear bubble that surrounded me since that first shocking talk in the doctor's office.

The first weeks after the bad news were hectic: I had to go through all sorts of tests before the surgery. I was also busy being scared to death. After all, my mother had died of cancer just a few years prior to my diagnosis. Although it was a different type of cancer, the fact was hardly reassuring. I was 37 and my younger daughter had just turned 5.

Looking back, I believe what helped me then was my previous experience with manifesting my dreams, a life-long reading obsession, my husband's full support, and a habit of questioning the "authorities" which is quite common in my generation of post-USSR immigrants. I started reading about alternative medicine and natural cancer remedies. And I soon realized that it was possible to remove cancer without the aggressive therapy, by changing the chemical processes in our body and creating an environment where cancer cells cannot survive. Yes, that meant changing my diet and lifestyle.

At the same time I was focusing all my energy on manifesting good health. Meditation, yoga, reiki and "The Secret" were my tools, along with visualization and make-shift techniques I created on the go.

I was still researching what would later become my alternative therapy when my doctor called. The pathology results came in and they found more cancer cells on the margins. Another shock, another round of self-pity and body-image-related fretting. Cancer was not only attacking my health, it was a threat to my identity, success, professional and social life. To make it worse, I was overwhelmed with fear, equally scared of cancer and cancer therapy. Neither seemed possible to survive. It was one of those moments when it looks easier to give up than to go on with your life. But I felt I had no choice. The stakes were too high and loosing was not an option.

On the day of mastectomy my mind was made up firmly: that was going to be the last invasive medical procedure I was willing to go through. I had been working on meditation and manifesting techniques since the initial diagnosis and the results were finally noticeable: fear was gone, I knew what I was doing and I knew how to do it. Instead of fighting cancer

Manifesting a New Life

I was moving towards the new healthy and happy me. My determination was so strong that I didn't need pain medication after the surgery - meditation and self-healing energy was enough to subdue the pain.

My life transformed little by little. The changes went deeper than simply changing the diet; I was developing a better understanding of what was good for me and what was to be removed from my life and from my kitchen. It is amazing how choosing the right foods and staying away from the wrong ones can be all it takes to reverse the metabolism back to normal and fix many health issues, including cancer.

What are the right and the wrong foods? The right ones are easy: lots of raw greens and vegetables, full of healing elements and enzymes. As for the wrong ones, many of them are taken for granted and can be found in any meal.

Sugar and simple carbs that turn into sugar inside our body increase acidity and damage the circulatory system. And since cancer cells feed and grow on sugar, it was the first thing to go away from my diet.

Animal-derived proteins, unlike vegetable proteins, provide the perfect tumor-building material and help the cancer grow. Eating vegan starves cancer cells and strengthens the immune system.

Gluten, a protein found in wheat, causes gut inflammation in most people. A lot of us also develop antibodies against gluten. All this interferes with the work of immune system which needs to be in top shape if you want to control cancer.

Toxins and preservatives found in packaged foods also help cancer grow, as cancer cells are happy to consume any metabolism waste. Staying away from most processed foods and learning about cleansing techniques will help the body eliminate the toxins faster.

Alcohol and caffeine are fine for healthy people if taken in moderation, but you don't want their effect on your system if you are fighting cancer.

Tumor thrives without oxygen while healthy cells need it to stay healthy. Make sure your cells get enough oxygen from regular physical activity and time spent outdoors.

Slowly but surely, I was moving away from toxic foods, toxic habits, and toxic relationships. Losing my once favorite foods wasn't easy in the beginning but got easier with time, as the toxins washed out of my body.

I understood one main thing: as long as I rely on someone else to make me healthy, I have no control over my life. The change is only strong enough when it comes from within.

There are lots of stories telling us about someone's "cancer journey". I choose to tell my story as the journey of health. My cancer diagnosis turned out to be a wake-up call. I am now stronger, healthier and happier than I ever was. And through this journey I discovered my life passion.

Manifesting a New Life

RAMZI CHEETY

Ramzi Cheety is a Director of Finance for a multinational company located in Montreal. Through his extensive knowledge in business and finance, Ramzi co-founded Free 2Bu, a coaching consulting company helping soul entrepreneurs excel in their business. He also co-created Free 2Bu Path, an eight week program that defines and clarifies your Path from a business and personal perspective. He helps individuals, through one-on-one or group coaching, to see through the clutter of life and achieve clarity, freedom and confidence. His deep spiritual connection is visible through his work especially the fusion of Finance & Spirituality.

www.Free2Bu.ca
www.Free2BuPath.com
www.facebook.com/rcheety
www.facebook.com/free2buprogramme
ramzi@free2bu.ca

CHAPTER 13

THE PATH TO SUCCESS STARTS WITH A LEAP OF FAITH

By Ramzi Cheety

In my private and group coaching sessions, I hear people say that they feel something inside of them but cannot verbalize it. They are looking for the "Thing". The "Thing" or their Life Purpose, so to speak that will change their lives and move them onto a prosperous Path.

The dilemma starts to brew when asked, what is your Life Path? "I don't know", they say.

This inner feeling is one of GRANDNESS. They don't know what exactly it is but they do know that they'd want to become someone or be like someone else.

Success is defined as achieving wealth, position and respect. It is also defined as achieving a goal or a target. Success is not about money. It is definitely not by the social status you achieve or the fancy cars, the big house, or designer clothes you own. Success is much deeper than the transient material stuff we associate ourselves with. Success is about the joy that emanates from deep within every time we complete the task at hand. That joy that arises from within is the joy of life, the joy of accomplishment. This feeling that we talk about is the true feeling of fulfillment.

"Success is not about doing what you love; Success is about loving what you do."

When you put your heart and soul in what you do, you create a positive energy that vibrates through every cell of your body. This energy or feeling will drive you to focus fully on the task at hand. The result is a happy, joyful and successful moment.

Here are the main five pillars of success:

Determination

Deep inside each and everyone is a fire that rest dormant until it matures. When the sensations start to rise, is when we start to embark on our new found Path. Some of us take this journey on a part time basis while others jump right in, head first, working relentlessly until they reap the reward of their successful venture. Determination means not giving up. It means that even if you do not achieve your goal, you still learn from your experiences and so you redefine and you realign your Path.

On the other hand, giving up means you failed, period. You cannot interpret giving up any other way. It means you are telling the Universe "I'm done". Kindly remove my name from the list of successful people as I have made a conscious decision to quit.

I've been wanting to publish a book for couple of years now. I do believe that I have a story to inspire and help people awaken to their life's essence. I cannot remember the number of so called books that I wrote. I've written on napkins, multiple write pads, on my computer and in emails that I send myself. None of what I wrote was inspiring to be published. Every manuscript I wrote gave me the courage and knowledge to write and re-write again and again until this one got published.

Set Clear and Precise GOALS

Where I work, I see people, including myself, walking in a zigzag movement between the parking lot and the entrance door. This year, the company painted a pedestrian walkway on the side of the street. Now, almost everyone walks within these lines till the front door. Until you have a precise goal in mind and a clear mission, you'll end up being pulled in different direction. Precision is a laser focused goal that you embark on.

Do ask yourself every now and then, WHY am I doing this? If the answer is for transient material, then drop what you're doing and refocus. Money is never the answer to success. Money is the outcome of a successful venture. Figure out exactly "WHY" you want to do what you do before you jump into it.

When my wife and I started Free 2Bu, we had great ideas but we were going in circles. These circles were actually taking us away from our "WHY". We thought we had it but in reality we were lost on the main aspect of our work. After consulting with a business coach, our vision became clearer and our focus became precise. From these consultations we came up with the phrase "We inspire you to use Spirituality when dealing with Emotional, Financial and Relationship matters.", that actually summed what we love to do. From that point on, we created the "Heart & Soul Café" a bi-weekly gathering, "Free 2Bu Path" an 8 week course that helps you pave the Path to your richness. After one of our Cafés a new segment was born Free 2Bu Kitchen whereby we help you achieve a balanced budget starting from your kitchen table. This allowed me to combine my cooking talent along with our Accounting and finance background to help people achieve a balanced budget and eat healthy meals.

Once you get your "WHY "and set your clear goals, then and only then your Path will be clearer.

Faith

Not only the WHY that clears your Path but also your belief in your ability to achieve your goals.

Do you feel that your knowledge is substandard to your peers? Do you feel that others can deliver better than you can? The poor little me story in our mind tends to make you believe and feel that others are better than you. Why is that? It's our underlying fear of failure and/or fear of criticism that manifests itself in different ways. When we start to believe in the "poor little me" story, and that usually happens fast, we start to act in that way.

When I started my journey on a spiritual Path, I found that I lacked some knowledge. I truly felt that others knew more than I did. One day, I attended a workshop given by someone that I looked up to. After the workshop, I start to chat with the attendees. To my shock, I found myself surrounded by everyone, including the presenter, listening intensely to what I had to say. Then I realized that my intense knowledge on the subject was just as adequate as anyone else including the presenter. My shortfall was my lack of belief in my ability to deliver rather than the knowledge that I acquired.

Self Confidence

Self confidence is an extension of Faith. How to overcome our fear of failure and replace it with self confidence?

Here's your homework, take a pen and paper and write:

1- A list of your Strength and weaknesses. This will give you a clearer picture of where you need to focus your attention.
2- Write your goals down, what do you intend to achieve and by when.
3- Write a promise to yourself to eliminate negative thoughts so you can believe in others the way you believe in yourself.

Read what you wrote every morning and every evening. This is one of the main pillars of the Law of Attraction. Use it wisely as positive thoughts will only generate positive results while the reverse will generate negative results.

NOWHERE, the hyphenated effect: No-where Vs Now-here

The hyphenated effect is what separates a successful venture from a non-successful one.

Now-Here is the act of being present in the moment. Being present gives us the ability to place all your attention on the task at hand. You are basically focused one thing only and that is the task at hand. This focus is generated by intense interest in your work which leads to intense enjoyment when you reach your goal. This is enthusiasm at its best.

No-Where means you are interested in your work but you are also focused on other life's issues. Or in simple word, multitasking. Basically, while you are focused on your work, you're also thinking on what's next on your to do list. The quality of your work will suffer in the process as you are rushing to get to the next task. The completion of your work has no meaning since it's a mean to get to next task. With this your current task become a burden and completing it becomes a huge task. This results in frustration, anger and also disappointments. The Karmic wheel of substandard outcomes and negative emotions against the present moment will persist in your life until you drop the future and become present.

Ask yourself every day, Am I Now-Here? Or Am I No-Where? Although the shortest distant between two points is a straight line, sometimes in life we have to detour and re-evaluate and re-align our strategy in order to reach our ultimate goal.

Failure is not a failure unless we label it so.

Sail through life with open arms embracing every life experience. Don't hold on to the past as it will tear your sail and ground you. Believe that you have succeeded and you'll realize that success has always been on your side.

Manifesting a New Life

THERESIA VALOCZY

I am a certified hypnotherapist and coach. In my work I help people to change their lives and manifest their dreams. I coach female and MLM enterpreneurs with business and artist start-ups and mentoring under 25 years old. I help my clients to discover and find their passion and grow their business, develop personality. My main aim is to teach people how to use their creativity energy and The Universal laws to complete their Life.

My published books:
Sprituality in Business, 2008, Hungary,
Women on the Fullfilment Way, 2013, Hungary

Website: www.sunrisedreamcoaching.com
Facebook: https://www.facebook.com/teraxlacio
Facebook: https://www.facebook.com/theresia.valoczy

CHAPTER 14

THE LIFE IF YOUR DANCE

By Theresia Valoczy

Have you ever felt that you needed a change? Chains complicate your life. You do not see a way to develop financially and emotionally. You expect something, but you do not know what it is. You know for sure: Something must be done...

Everything has a reason. Perhaps, at the moment we do not know what the purpose of those reasons are. We are looking for answers that the outside world does not conform too.

Because the answer is within you.

How to get a positive outcome of a negative event? How to manifest a new Life?

A year ago, I suffered from writer's block. I felt trapped in my life. I lost my balance and ran out of energy. I was crushed financially and emotionally. I began to take stock of my past. I analyzed my life. I asked, and I answered truthfully. My soul has become easier, but it was a pain in within.

One afternoon when I felt I had enough, I meditated in my herbs garden. Once I calmed down, I let my thoughts flow. I was in the moment.

Accept it into your heart! - Came the idea- Embrace with Love!

All events are related to each other. They are born from each other and hugging each other to become a whole. Change a thought and your world will change. Put it in your heart and it will develop into love. Accept and embrace!

I believe in positive thinking. I teach this. This is the main theme of my books. However, it was difficult at the moment. I focused on the past and was stuck in it.

My mother said to me, when I was a child, "Your Life is your Dance. Not all the same kind of dance. If your dance has a passion, your life is nice, fulfilled and happy. If your Dance doesn't have love and passion, you'll be tired and world-weary. You make a decision, always. Do you live in the dance or let drain the manifest of your hands?" Her words live deep within me, revitalizing and pushing me back in the flow.

Started to open up to the world, I began to understand the importance of ideas. Everything around me has become easier. I felt for the first time in a long while that I had arrived.

My world was Peace. Accept in your Heart! Embrace with Love! Do you believe in love? Do you believe in the power of the Heart, which converts everything?

Manifesting a New Life

Everything is energy. What you think about is what you get back. Like attracts like. The decision is always in your hands. You danced the dance of your life. You dictate the rhythm.

Everything that happens leaves an imprint in you. Your energy system, chakras, your heart, body and mind remembers what happened in your life. The subconscious mind accepts everything. The pain, fear, despair, sadness, anger is stored in your body, mind and aura. It comes to life, without you wanted it too. Again and again repeats itself.

Do you know any stories about a similar situations that occur annually in people's lives? Similar relationships over and over again. Recurring financial Stories. Child-rearing problems. In your life do you have a recurring event, a feeling?

I have good news! Not only will the negative experience be stored in your mind and body. All positive feelings and experiences also makes an impression in you. All positive rays. It gives rhythm to your Dance.

When you feel tired, stalled, you desire a new life, at the moment to make changes. Keep in mind:

All feelings and thoughts emit a signal to the Universe. Regardless, if this signal is good or bad, the Universe reflects it. What you think is what you get. This is a Universal Law.
   If you change your reaction, the result will change. When you feel something is blocking your manifestation, stand up,

breathe deeply and smile! Accept in your Heart your experiences! Embrace and Love!

On the day I let the thoughts create balance in myself, I swam with the flow. I felt my power. I was more confident than the previous day. I realized that what I went through is meaningful. It made me who I am. My dreams and desires were awakened, and I had received huge zest. I existed again.

The Teraxlation was born.

Teraxlation is a Manifest Method. This includes energy and chakras healing, releasing emotional blocks, trans breathing and hypnotherapy. This is very simple, powerful and effective. Have you got a dream? Would you like your dreams come true? Would you like to experience the State of Natural Wholeness?

I really wanted too.

My thoughts flowed in the small garden.

My breathing changed. I took a deep breath in through the crown chakra. I drove down along the spine and I exhaled through the root. I repeated it three times. Every slow and deep breath opens my mind and every release clears my chakras and energy system. It unlocks my blocks and emancipates emotions. I felt good.

I started thinking about why I'm grateful for my life. I left the crippling thoughts that one could not cope. This was the feeling of worthlessness. I focused on the good and the beautiful. But, that feeling was still there deep inside me. I closed my eyes, and I said, "I am grateful for this feeling, I know this taught me something. Accept your Heart! Embrace and Love!"

The thought came again.

The Heart is the central of our Life and central of our Body. This is very important. Our dreams live in our heart. When we feel Gratitude for something, our Heart is happy and opens the door to the opportunities.

My block was feeling of worthless. I was grateful for it, but only slightly eased. Then I understood the idea: the heart has got the transforming power. What you put into your heart this dissolves. If I receive the negative feelings in my heart, these may develop from negative to positive? If I embrace and love my blocks, negative emotions, negative circumstances, will this changes? Wow!

What happens if I put my positive events in my heart? It comes to life with a passion, and everything becomes feasible! Yes!

Try it! This is my Love Meditation, the based on the Teraxlation:

Please close your eyes, and take a nice deep breath. Breathe in

and breathe out slowly. Relax. Breath in through your Crown
Chakra, drive down along the spine, and exhale slowly
though your root. Repeat three times. Every deep inhalation
open the way for the energies of the Divine Self and each slow
exhalation cleans the energy channel. Focus on your Heart.

Feel the rhythm! Connect it! Your heart is home to your
dreams. Feel it. Relax...

Put your hands on your Heart. Feel the rhythm. Love it! Enjoy
it! Be thankful for his music, his voice. Be thankful for your

life. Please repeat: I LOVE YOU. I LOVE YOU. I LOVE YOU.

This sentence is full of happiness, joy and feeling good. Think
of a person who is important to you. Imagine at...I LOVE
YOU. I LOVE YOU. I LOVE YOU.

Think yourself and imagine that your dream can comes

true...See it! Feel it! Imagine it! When your energy focuses on
your dream, please repeat: I LOVE YOU. I LOVE YOU: I
LOVE YOU. Enjoy this moment, than take a deep breath and
open your eyes.

Remember! You make a decision! Your thoughts may help or
obstruct your manifesting process.

This method can transforms your feelings, negative events,
and grow the wonderful moments. The Love Meditation
helps grow your inner-peace, improves your self-awareness,
develops into your personality, opens your Heart to Gratitude
and Love, manifest your dreams, clears your emotions and

thoughts.

Imagine what happens when this becomes a habit? Conscious changes, instinctively...

This exercise removed my writer's block. Missing the little devil that lived in my soul. My dream has come true with a little extra help.

What is the Extra?

I combined the Love Meditation with the Affirmation. This helps regain my financial balance.

When you use this Love Meditation before going to sleep, your mind opens the Inner Voice and Deep Calm. Is this state of unconscious, and your subconscious mind is the Boss.

When you're relaxed, repeat or listen to money affirmation.

You can make audio recordings...

For example: I manifest whatever I need or desire. I am wealthy in every possible way. I attract the very best of everything. I am powerful money-magnet. I attract prosperity quickly and easily.

For best results, use for at least 21 days.

When you wake up and you have a good idea in your mind

(please!) take on action!

One year has passed. Every day I apply the method. My life in balance. I learned to love my life and my style of writer. I understood the situation and what I experienced. I know that every dream can come true. Every problem can be solved in the hope of a new life. Live in the possibility! Accept in your Heart all positive and negative events, and Embrace! Use your magic wand, change your reaction and your dreams into reality. Manifesting a New Life! You Deserve it!

I believe in you.

Manifesting a New Life

LIZ SMART, N.D.

Would you like to take charge of your physical and emotional health? Liz Smart is passionate about inspiring people to live they're best life. Leveraging her close to 20 years as a Health Facilitator and Naturopath, she teaches invaluably simple tools to cleanse and rebuild your body to experience optimal health. Claim the life you truly desire by discovering the power of how pivotal your mind plays a role in your well being. Discover techniques that you can implement that will give you back your inherent right to Manifesting your New Life

Following her true mission of helping people find they're peace, Liz hosts Travelling Health Retreats.

Blessed with surprise twin daughters, Liz has the pleasure being, sharing, teaching and travelling with.

Liz Smart is a Naturopath, Certified Trainer at Infinite Possibilities, Health Facilitator, Colon Hygienist, Senior Director at The Wellness Company, Speaker, Co-Author and Singer. You may contact Liz at Website : www.lizsmart.com Email : liz@lizsmart.com Telephone : (514) 793-4394 Facebook: https://www.facebook.com/liz.lizsmart Twitter: https://twitter.com/1LizSmart Linkedin: https://www.linkedin.com/in/smartliz

CHAPTER 15

I LOVE MY LIFE! I AM A CREATOR!

By Liz Smart, N.D.

Ohhhh life is good! I have this happy ball inside me, that's
how I've always described it. I feel like I'm destined for
greatness. There's a deep passion for life within me that
makes me feel like I'm going to pop! I just get so excited. I
feel I can do anything, be anything. Then one day, it was
gone. Where did it go? I lost myself. I couldn't recognize
myself anymore. Where did that happy go lucky, always
bubbly, smiling Liz go? Looking back, it feels like I was
swallowed up into some Vortex. It took me years to figure it
out.

Now it's all come full circle.

It's been scary for me to expose myself in this way. What will
people think? What about my parents? I do not wish to hurt
them, they are from a different generation and people did not
speak of these things. How will people look at me? How
about you? That's really what it's all about, why I'm writing
this. My wish here is for you to feel liberated. My purpose is
to help you be free and find peace, as I have. Know that you
too can Be-Do-Have all you desire and dream, even if an event
may have gotten in the way of you living freely. In my
experience, you can have peace, even amongst the chaos. No

matter how long it takes.

I was abused when I was 5 years old and it went on into my 20's. It was a close friend of the family who became my godfather. The dynamics of an abusive relationship is quite the emotional spider web. There was so much mental manipulation going on, and in my case years of physical improprieties, but mostly psychological warfare. Due to this abuse I learnt to put up a front. Everything on the outside had to look good, because low and behold, god forbid, someone would see the truth. I finally told my mother my secret. It came out in a heated exchange, after I hinted to something and she pried it out of me with just the right questions. I felt it was something that kept me from being fully understood by her. It pained me so much to tell her, but from that moment on we became even closer. I'm not going to lie and say that my "coming out" went smoothly. There are wounds that would seem impossible to mend. Not only did I live with the abuse, I was the one who came out and shook things up in my family. For years I felt as if I had a Scarlett letter on my forehead and still feel like an outsider when it comes to some members of my immediate family. Why am I telling you this? I made a promise to myself that I would be brutally honest, real, raw and guided divinely on what to share.

We all have our demons, don't we? No matter the demons, getting to the point where we can say, "ok I finally get it and now I choose me, once and for all" while still being able to take care of the people around me, standing up for my life, my passions, my mission and by adding value to my own life, I can in turn add value to others.

This being said, the mind just wants to protect itself. I remind myself to live in Love versus Fear. We cannot live in both. For example, part of me questioned my purpose for writing this and my mind automatically, after years of doing so wanted to go back to a place of fear and perhaps even sabotage. So reminding myself to choose love over fear makes it is easier to trust that all is divine, all is well. I wholeheartedly wish that my story inspire others to feel the same liberation I do.

I met my husband in 1995. We had our share of issues, and now that we have distance, I have clarity. I was so in love with this man, the end of our union still brings tears to my eyes. Where to begin?

Remember my happy ball? This is where I lost it. There is no place for blame. Blame is a poison. It serves no one and only brings you farther from taking full responsibility for your life and being blissfully happy. We did the best we could with what we had. Boy, did we each bring our own share of baggage. My greatest wish for him is that he find Peace in his heart. A long overdue crossroad had come about where we each had to go our own way. I know now that PEACE is worth its weight in gold. There is no room in second guessing ourselves. Regret serves no purpose.

The full picture makes sense now. I found my path due to our union. If it hadn't been for our dysfunctional relationship I may not have had reason to study the works of Louise Hay 20 years ago and become a Health Facilitator and Naturopath. I see how I settled for fleeting moments versus a lifetime of delicious memories. The pain, the sadness, the loss of self serves a purpose in the larger scheme of things. I can use my past as a tool to help others. I was no longer being my true self. I realized the reason I stayed in this relationship for so long was because I had been programmed from a very young age to act as if all was well; I was conditioned to put up with all the nonsense and go on with my life. Although I can be very outspoken, whatever I was saying somehow held no weight. I felt I had no voice. I was dismissed. I began to believe I must be the root of the problem or just plain CRAZY! My two most precious gifts came from our marriage; the blessing of what I like to call our surprise twin daughters. One thing is for certain, he is an amazing father who absolutely adores them. I used this to justify staying in a marriage that had been problematic from the beginning and dead for many years.

He took care of us financially so I chose to put my career on hold, staying home to raise and homeschool our daughters. I found my greatest joy being with them and am filled with a deep sense of pride that I am able to offer an extension to their childhood innocence. The girls and I start each morning by putting on some relaxing music each taking turns to say our affirmations and gratitude.

The children were becoming more independent so on a part time basis I began marketing health and wellness and was rather quickly able to create a successful business. This gave me the opportunity to find myself again. My happy ball came back! I saw how I was adding value to other people's lives and it gave me such fulfillment. It was a character building time in our marriage. We stayed together with the commitment that he join me in a transformational weekend. That was the defining factor for me to stay, because I had started to realize how I no longer needed to compromise

145

myself by staying in an unhappy marriage. I believed, especially for the children's sake, I should make 1 last effort to make this marriage work. I choose to look at the weekend as a chance for a fresh start, hoping that this time we set aside would solidify it. A few days prior, he backed out. I couldn't believe it! It was at that moment when my children turned to me and said "Mommy, you deserve to be happy, you should get a divorce." Wow! Right out of the mouths of babes! I felt I was given permission. All that time, I had stayed, enduring it for my daughters when in reality I was hiding, afraid to take full responsibility for my life. I was using my daughters as an excuse. I immediately became aware and made the decision that instead of using my situation as a place to hide, I needed to set an example once and for all: take a stand in my life and end this marriage!

I felt the weight of the world melt off my shoulders. I went to the event on my own, it was one of the most cathartic times in my life. I had developed so many fears while living under the radar, even the 6 hour drive all alone scared me. I came face to face with who I had become and I no longer wanted to live this lie. I let go of the fear in my head, the pain in my heart, the anger in my stomach and came home with a quiet resolve that I had not known in years, if ever. I sat down calmly with my husband and explained how we needed to separate for the good of the children and stop exposing them to our dysfunctional exchanges. We both agreed and from that moment, Magical Manifestations came flooding my way. I took a refresher course in Naturopathy, re-instated my license as a Colon Hygienist, became a Certified Trainer with Mike Dooley, and began teaching the course Infinite Possibilities:

The Art of Changing Your Life. New clients came flowing my way. Business ventures open up to me. I even brought my daughters on vacation on my own. Just to name a few, it was amazing how many generous gifts came my way in such a short period of time. I was and am still filled with gratitude. In an instant everything had changed. It all fell into place with such ease and grace. I was free to watch my light shine bright. I remembered I was a powerful being.

I had all I needed to MANIFEST A NEW LIFE. I began living the life of my dreams.

I had come full circle. It will take the time it takes, step by step. Be patient with yourself, no judgment, all is as it should be. You may discover, like me, "it only takes 1 day, 1 second in time, 1 friend, 1 dream, 1 leap of faith to change everything forever" I love my life! I am a creator!!

Manifesting a New Life

JANE "TRAINER JANE" WARR

Jane "Trainer Jane" Warr is the acclaimed author of "The 3 Minute Workout: How to Lose Your Muffin Top, Thunder Thighs and Other Jiggly Bits" now in prepublication. Serving thousands of clients over the past two decades as a Personal Trainer & Nutrition Coach, she specializes in Vitruvian Training.

She has expanded her professional practice to include communications through her Lifestyle coaching program "Find Your Voice" and as a "Verbal Aikido" Authorized Business Partner. From feeling voiceless herself in the past, Jane is passionate about inspiring others to speak their truth and committed to your transformation. She now travels the globe to share her powerful message of finding your voice and using it!

www.TrainerJaneSays.com

CHAPTER 16

STOP AND SMELL THE ROSES

By Jane "Trainer Jane" Warr

Writing this chapter has transformed me. It has revealed to me the many profound lessons that I have been taught throughout the past year. I have heard myself call 2015 painful, yet profound. The process of writing this has pulled those past thoughts and feelings, as well as so many new ones, together. I am grateful for the lessons I have received and the opportunity to share them with you today.

In January, I was introduced to "Verbal Aikido" by James MacNeil, Author & Founder. It isn't often you come across something so impactful to both business and personal growth that you feel a need to share it with the world, but indeed I did. Immediately, I decided to become an Authorized Business Partner and I am excited to share Verbal Aikido with you and empower you to take your relationships to new heights!

Verbal Aikido turned out to be the catalyst to all the wonderful experiences of mine over the last seven months. It led to an amazing self-awareness and it further allowed my business to skyrocket too. Coined the Art and Science of Communications, it dives deep into both and provides a profound understanding of interpersonal relationships at every level, in every situation.

Wouldn't you agree that the highest of highs and lowest of low moments of your life had other people involved? Therefore learning to communicate honestly, openly, respectfully, and directly, ensuring the other party feels heard, understood, accepted and respected is paramount! It may sound simple, and don't we all do that already, in our daily exchanges with family, friends, coworkers, and ourselves? No!

Of course there is much more to it, but the point is that it opened my eyes to visualizing and wanting greater things for myself, my family, my business, and all the lives I touch. It revealed to me that no relationship is impossible, and that I could therefore choose to save difficult relationships, build new needed relationships, envision a better me, and a new life! In difficult conversations, I can respect the other party's energy, redirect their energy, and maintain my balance. I have connected heart-to-heart with individuals I assure you I would not have otherwise. That is how lives are impacted and transformed. This is liberating!

Though I always believed myself to be introspective, self-aware, respectful and genuine, I now think differently about each situation, each conversation, and the other individual with which I choose to have a meaningful connection. As I bring a calm confidence and safe congruent strength in character, rapport is built. Failing this, love is lost, friendships lost, and business relationships end.

It is incredible how dramatically, easily, and quickly my relationships have improved. "Transformational" and "life changing" is the least I can say about my Verbal Aikido communication skills. Conversations that may have been difficult in the past, are now free of heightened emotions, my buttons aren't being pushed, and we are speaking rationally, truly communicating. There is no winner or loser in the end, but a win-win. I have a very small family, so every relationship is of tremendous importance to me. There are treasures in every relationship! I am forever changed and it is with tremendous excitement that I share this passion with others.

Instead of focusing on lack in my relationships and all the past mistakes and pains, I now focus on how I can take responsibility in improving my own ability to communicate, control myself, and manage my interactions to thereby influence others.

We attract more of what we are, and I am a better me!

Understanding that we cannot change others, nor is it our place to do so, we need to start with ourselves. Meditating on the word "grace" I learned to calm myself, and accept myself and all the good or bad that was going on around me, with a sense of peace not felt before. As my self-talk improved, I grew kinder and more compassionate towards myself, finding more self-love. Today, I live Verbal Aikido. I continue to study it, and proudly share it with others through one-on-one coaching, public workshops, and corporate speaking.

All this positivity and personal development brought me back to using affirmations and declarations daily.

My favourite affirmation:

"Everything that is mine by divine right is coming to me now, rightly, freely, speedily. I am receiving now."
- CATHERINE PONDER

In February I went on a writing trip to Cuba, expecting to work and relax. I find oceans meditative, and my favourite and the most powerful part of nature to be inspired by. I found myself spending time standing or kneeling in the shallow water, just pondering life. I was contemplating the direction I wanted it to take, was affirming it would take, asking for it, praying for it, and allowing myself to be open to receive all the greatness available to me.

Conversations I had with others all seemed to be in perfect alignment with my dreams and goals. I had revelations about where I was holding myself back in life, and found clarity as to how I should proceed. I realized why an important project remained incomplete and I felt the "ah-ha", in the moment! It was the breakthrough so desperately needed. Sometimes people and opportunities present themselves to us to provide these lessons, and we need to slow down long enough to hear them.

Upon my return, I wrote a list of character traits I valued. I had come home with such clarity of purpose and desires!

In April my family suffered the loss of someone very dear to us. The profound grief that overwhelmed me felt all-consuming. The death was so dramatic, so quick, and so unfair. It was devastating and hurt so many.

I do believe everything happens for a reason. Everyone comes

Manifesting a New Life

into our lives at a certain time for a certain reason, and we
must find the lessons offered to us from these experiences. I
had to fill a role I never expected to need to fill, and felt
emotions and pain that most did not understand. As
something so woeful could not be expected nor planned for, I
chose to manifest our strength, courage, and the love to get us
all through it. It certainly took me using healthy
communication, respect, patience, meditation and affirmations
that we would all get through the saddest of days together,
and hopefully grow stronger and closer.

The beauty in the loss was the new and renewed friendships
that followed. The heartwarming kindness was nothing less
than awesome! The closeness and connection I felt was
powerful, and something for which I will be eternally grateful.
I decided. I chose to work on the relationships without fear
and apprehension. I knew my heart was in the right place,
continuously affirming that peace would be restored in our
lives.

Reflecting on the powerful relationships and life lessons of
this year, I created here an exhaustive list of character traits I
feel have especially been speaking to me, and leading me.
They are in no particular order.

My wish if for you to resonate with some of them; chew on
them. Read through this section slowly and mindfully. Let
them sink in. Stop and allow yourself to feel them if they give
you reason to pause.

> independence, joy, abundance, acceptance, release,
> gratitude, self-respect, closeness, trust, openness,
> vulnerability, empathy, caring, safety, intuition,

helpful, dependable, mature, deep, willing,
partnership, equality, respect, grace, love, faith, hope,
sympathy, empathy, humility, intimacy, passion,
ambitious, security, loving, honouring, calm,
demonstrative, direct, admirable, introspective,
visionary, clarity, loyal, stable, articulate, caring,
thoughtful, emotional, strong, courageous, free,
teachable, coachable, friendship, determined, inspiring,
encouraging, insightful, forgiving, compassionate,
persistent, focused, clear, curiosity, possibility,
positivity, giving, sharing, communicative, successful,
proud, confident, hopeful, dependable, protective,
thankful, appreciative, generous, romantic, patient,
committed, optimistic, challenging

One night in May, I had a dream like no other. I awoke
startled and overwhelmed with a vision and message running
through my mind. I grabbed paper and pen and quickly wrote
down anything that was coming to me. The words "Find Your
Voice" came through loud and clear. It wasn't just a message
for me to consider, but came with a vision of me speaking
from stage with this message for the world to hear! It was so
surreal, resonating throughout me for days to come.

With the title of Find Your Voice, I have launched my Lifestyle
Coaching program. I help individuals set and achieve their
significant goals, find their clarity of purpose, live it, and voice
it! I find the courageous individuals coming to me have been
holding back in their lives, for much of their lives. They have
held back on some simple things, biting their tongue for fear
of judgement, or sometimes holding in what they most desire
to share with their friends and family, or the world! They
don't feel like they have a voice, or the confidence to speak up.

Manifesting a New Life

They too have greatness within them, that they want so
desperately to share with others, and feel heard. It is my
heart's desire to help serve them.

I can empathize with what they are going through, and relate
to their experiences. Growing up as the shy one, the introvert,
speaking only when spoken to, I learned to hold back or hold
in much of what I was thinking. Sadly, until a few years ago, I
was still doing the same.

It was through training and coaching that I began to see things
differently, better. I could see myself in my clients and started
to challenge myself to find new ways of speaking up,
speaking my truth, and not fearing the consequences. I won't
say it wasn't difficult or that I have mastered it. It is, however,
work that is so worth doing. Choosing to learn and willing to
get out of my comfort zone helps me to grow. It doesn't serve
anyone to play small.

Meditating on the word Belief has helped me to believe in
myself. I have the honour of paying forward what I have
learned to others. Everyone has greatness within them. YOU,
have greatness within you!

I am forever grateful to everyone who has helped me to grow,
and for every life lesson that has been presented to me. I
didn't have control over the occurrences, but learned to
control my emotions and responses with Verbal Aikido. I have
learned new ways to communicate my message using Verbal
Aikido through my Find Your Voice program, and believe it
to be what gave me the strength to overcome my fears and
come forward to voice my message to you. I believe I

manifested a new life because of my willingness to deal with it all, with grace. The new, happier me is leaving a positivity wake all around me.

I have taken the time to look back and reflect over the past months and to celebrate along the way. I have strength, a voice, and a message I didn't have just a few short months ago.

My wish for you is to take chances, as they are worth taking. Fail forward, and find your voice. Go out and sing! Karaoke is a great way to get out of your comfort zone!

Affirm and declare all that you wish for yourself and your loved ones. Make a list of what you want to receive in your life. You have infinite potential within you to manifest all of your heart's desires. Be open to it! Manifest it. Expect it. See it. Feel it. Believe it. Affirm it. Declare it. Focus on it. Visualize it. Live it. Love it. Smile! Rejoice and be glad in it! Find your voice! Speak it into existence! Sing it out loud! Receive it and Accept it.

Then celebrate it! It is in that state of pure joy that I believe you will find all that you desire. Take the time, and take the chance. You are worth it! Stop and smell the roses. I can, and I do!

Manifesting a New Life

Dedicated to: SWAMJMPWWVJVDW

Verbal Aikido
By James MacNeil, Author & Founder

To learn more about Verbal Aikido
visit VerbalAikido.com
or TrainerJaneSays.com

PATRICIA LEBLANC, RMT, IARP

Patricia LeBlanc inspires and motivate others to manifest their goals and dreams. Patricia is passionate about helping others to live a happy and abundant life. Using a holistic approach, she helps her clients to get out of their own way and she teaches them how to manifest their goals, dreams and desires into their life.

Patricia is an Award Winning Author, Speaker, Certified Abundance Attraction Coach, Registered Reiki Master Teacher, Certified Integrated Energy Therapy® (IET®) Master Instructor, and Certified Angel Card Reader. She is also trained and certified in ThethaHealing® and Realm Readings.

You can contact Patricia via:
Business Phone: 1-647-977-6987
Email: info@patricialeblanc.ca
Website: www.patriciaeleblanc.com
Website: www.manifestinganewlife.com

CHAPTER 17

HOW TO LIVE A HAPPY AND ABUNDANT LIFE!

By Patricia LeBlanc, RMT, IARP

There is a lot of talk about Abundance. A lot people think that abundance is only having more than enough money in their life. But, that is so not true. You should be abundant in all areas of your life.

What is Abundance? Abundance is when you have more than enough of whatever it is that you want. You can have an abundance of Love. You can have an abundance of friendship. You can have an abundance of opportunities. You can have an abundance of money. You can have an abundance of fun. You can have an abundance of food. You can even have an abundance of good deeds. You can have an abundance of energy. You can create an abundance of time for yourself. You can also have an abundance of spirituality in your life.

Basically you can have an abundance of anything that exits on this planet. It is not limited to having lots of money. In fact, you should not just focus on the money or financial aspects of your life. Yes, it is very important to have money as it takes money to enjoy life but, it should never be your only focus.

Focus on what you love and abundance will follow.
You should always do what brings you joy while providing

value for any products and/or services you provide. You should focus on living a balanced, happy and abundant life. What is a balanced life, you may think? For me a balanced life is when you focus not just on work/business but also focus on your health, personal time, building relationships with others. You also need to make sure to get your sleep. In order to live a happy and abundant life, it is very important to believe that you are truly abundant. It is important to be abundant and more important have fun during the whole process.

Here are some of my tips about how to attract more abundance in your life. Remember there is more than enough abundance to go around for everyone. So never hold yourself back as you are afraid to take abundance from anyone else. The only person you take from is yourself. Play big and dream big.

Focus on abundance and not on the lack or scarcity.

A lot of people focus on what they do not have. Perfect example is money. A lot of people will focus on the fact that they have a lack of money, and then wonder why they do not get more. They will keep telling themselves I have no money. I have lots of debt. I am broke, etc…

According to the law of attraction, what you focus on, you will attract more of. So stop focusing on what you do not have and start focusing on what you have. If you do not have money, stop focusing on it. Start focusing that you have an abundance of money instead of focusing that you are broke or have no money. With time, you will start manifesting more money. Start thinking that you have an abundance of love, health, money, energy, or whatever you want to manifest.

Manifesting a New Life

Remember you can have an abundance of anything that you want as there is more than enough for everyone. The only person stopping you is you! So make it a point starting today, to focus on only abundance instead of the lack. Watch the magic start happening.

Appreciate and be grateful for what you currently have.

It is very important to be grateful for every single thing, opportunity and person that you have in your life. Also make certain that you appreciate all the small things. I count my blessings every single and say thank you to the Universe for having a roof on top of my head. For having food on the table. For having amazing people in your life. For waking up breathing this morning. I also say thank you Universe for bringing forth a brand new day and I am looking forward to open all of the gifts that you will be sending my way.

When you are going through a hard time, focus on what life lesson are you meant to learn. Be grateful for that amazing experience as it will allow you to grow and become a better person. I now know I needed to go through all of my many life challenges to help other people live a better life. I am now grateful for those experiences as they made me the person that I am. But I can tell you at times, I was not grateful and in fact was really angry. Guess what, when I was able to shift my anger to gratefulness and learn the life lesson, my life got much better. I was able to attract abundance into my life.

You also want to keep a gratitude journal. Write in your journal every single day. This is even more important when you are going through a life challenge. I even spend time reading my gratitude journal when I am going through a life challenge. 99.9% of the time, it makes me realize how lucky and blessed that I am. It helps me to shift my energy back to full of abundance. It may take time to bounce back up but it will help me get back to an energy of gratefulness much quicker.

Remember you always have something to be grateful for. You just need to find it!

Choose to develop your abundance mentality.

If you want to be abundant, you need to start believing it. You also need to believe that you are worthy of living an abundant life. I have a list of affirmation that I use to help me with this. Here is a list of my favorite abundance affirmation that I use every single day: * I am abundant. * Abundance flows to me and is around me. I am surrounded by abundance. * I am provided for today, and all of my tomorrows to come. * I always have whatever I need. The Universe takes good care of me. * My Life is full of love and joy and all the material things that I need. * I allow all good things to come into my life and I enjoy them. * I love abundance and prosperity and I attract it naturally. * Abundance and prosperity is my birthright and I have it. * I am in a state of fulfillment, have abundant love and joy into my life and I am free to do whatever I wish to do. * My job/business is an all-consuming love affair and I attract whatever I need through it. * I am prosperous, healthy, happy and live in abundance. * I am thankful for the abundance and prosperity in my life.

Take the affirmations that resonate with you and start using them. You can also create your own Affirmations.

You can also read books in the field of abundance. One of my favorite books include "Think and Grow Rich" by Napoleon Hill. This is a book that you will want to invest in and read several times a year. Every single time that I read this book, I learn something new. Another book that I love is Jack Canfield's The Success Principles. I love how easy it is to read but also that it includes that you need to be successful in life in all areas of your life. Remember, it is important to focus in all areas of your life. I was also very fortunate to have seen him speak live and he is simply amazing. I also have several books from my Mentor, Dr. Joe Vitale which includes The Attractor Factor and the Awakening Course, to name a few.

If you do not like to read, then guess what you can watch videos or listen to audios books. When I am writing I will listen to videos a lot. Some of the videos that I will watch are: anything by Robin Sharma, Tony Robbins, and Dr. Joe Vitale, just to name a few. I know that Dr. Joe Vitale also has audio programs. I have several of his programs and I can tell you that if you apply them, they work. Make it a point to invest at least 20 minutes a day to read, listen to audios or videos that will help your mindset. I actually find at least two to three hours a day, but a minimum of 20 minutes is a great start.

Surrender yourself with people who live a happy and abundant life.

It is very important to surrender yourself with like-minded people. You want to be around people who believe that anything is possible. If the people who are part of your inner circle, do not believe that you can be abundant, then you need to find new people. If you are looking for an abundance of love, then make certain the people around you come from love. You can join meetups or groups of like-minded people who want to achieve the same goals and dreams.

Make an inventory of people in your life. Start by making a list of people in your life, family members, friends, colleagues, and acquaintances. Go through your list. When you are with this person, either in person or on phone/skype, do you feel joy most time that you are with them? Do they help make you a better person? Do they support you and encourage you to go after your goals and dreams? If the answer is no most or all the time, you need to limit your time with them or blessed them and release them from your life. You may be wondering, what happens if they are family members. You will either need to learn to block their negative energy and limit your time spent with them or release them from your life.

You and only YOU know which one is best for you.

Create your days with abundance in mind.

It is important to spend your time doing things that you love to do and with people you love. You see when you vibrate at a higher energy, you will be able to manifest more abundance into your life. If I have tasks that I need to complete that I don't like to do. I do them first. After that I can focus on my happy tasks. My day is better and it keeps in an abundance energy. Make time every day to spend me time. Make a list of what you love to do and divide them in 2 categories: free or low cost and then costs money. So now you have no excuse not doing what you love.

Manifesting a New Life

Keep reminding yourself and keep looking for reminders.

It is very important to keep reminding yourself that you are
abundant. I filled out several small green index cards which
I wrote on them: I am abundant. My life is full of abundance
in all areas of my life. I live a happy and abundant life. I have
placed them in my wallet, every purse and bag that I owe.
On the board beside my office space, my bed, my lounge area.
I look at it several times a day. By counting your blessings,
you are manifesting abundance into your life. Make it a point
to keep your gratitude journal as this will help you keep
looking for abundance. I cannot stress enough the importance
of keeping a gratitude journal.

What I love about Abundance is that you can create
abundance in every areas of your life. In fact, I would say,
that it is very important to focus in all areas of your life.
Your professional/business life, personal life, lifestyle,
health, relationships, emotional, spiritual life. If you do not
feel abundant in all areas, start with one area and work your
way to all areas of your life. You are worthy and deserve to
live a happy and abundant life.

When you create abundance, it is easy and flows as long as
you are in alignment with yourself. Go with the flow and
think, feel and act abundant. Watch the magic start
happening. Remember there is more than enough abundance
for everyone. You were meant to live a happy and abundant
life and not struggle through life. Start today to live a happy
and abundant life. Once you make the decision it will become
easier each day to be happy and abundant.
Happy Manifesting!

CONCLUSION

As I write this, I am thinking about how blessed that I am. I have found the most incredible co-authors and their chapters are inspiring. I am blessed that I have manifested the life that I always wanted but never had the courage to do so. I am so grateful that I did not let life challenges hold be back.

After reading my co-authors chapters, I realized that every single one of them have created a new life at one point of their life. They have all overcome life challenges and created a better life. They have gone thru various transformation to get to where they now are.

I hope that you have enjoyed reading all of the amazing chapters in this book. I hope that you now realize that you are in control of your life. That you have the power to manifesting the life that you truly want.

If any of my co-authors chapters, including my own, resonated with you, please reach out to them or me to see how we can help you manifest a new life.

Always remember there is enough abundance for everyone. You are worthy of living a happy and abundant life. You have the power of manifesting anything that you truly want.

Happy Manifesting!
Patricia LeBlanc, RMT, IARP
#1 International Best Selling Author
Certified Abundance Attraction Coach

Manifesting a New Life

Patricia LeBlanc, RMT, IARP

Guidance, Inspiration, Motivation
Learn how to get out of your own way and how to
manifest your goals and dreams.

www.patriciaeleblanc.com and manifestinganewlife.com

Patricia LeBlanc's Free Gift:

20 minute of free abundance attraction coaching session or free 20 minute Integrated Energy Therapy (IET) Session upon purchase of Manifesting a New Life! Submit your proof of purchase and email address at info@patricialeblanc.ca

Join my Manifesting a New Life Facebook Group at https://www.facebook.com/groups/ManifestingaNewLife for more ressources on manifesting.

HOW CAN I HELP YOU?

My mission in life is to help you manifest the life that you want while living a happy and abundant life. I want to help you discover what you truly want and help you get out of your own way. Call me at 647-977-6987 or email me at info@patricialeblanc.ca to see how I can help you like I have done for over one thousand people before you.

Patricia xo
Patricia LeBlanc, RMT, IARP
6 Times International Best Selling Author, Certified Abundance Attraction Coach, Registered Reiki Master Teacher and Certified IET Master Instructor